CW00517138

Dear Reader,

The book that you hold in your hands is not like the others. It has been produced through a print-on-demand system. This means that your copy was packaged right for you, following your order. It is not one in a million, left it there waiting for someone to buy it; it is *yours*. We therefore apologize if you had to put up with some minor discomfort, if you had to deal with shipping costs or to wait longer than expected; on the other hand, this print and distribution system has allowed you to buy a book - your book - that other publishers, linked to traditional systems, would have considered useless to reprint. We, on the contrary, in doing so we give you the chance to read it.

We greet and thank you for buying from Edizioni Trabant and we hope to see you on the pages of another volume.

Good reading.

Edizioni Trabant

Isbn 978-88-96576-45-8

Edizioni Trabant 2014 - Brindisi (Italy)
www.edizionitrabant.it
redazione@edizionitrabant.it

Louise Mack

A Woman's Experiences
in the Great War

Edizioni
Trabant

Louise Mack
(courtesy of Mitchell Library,
State Library of New South Wales)

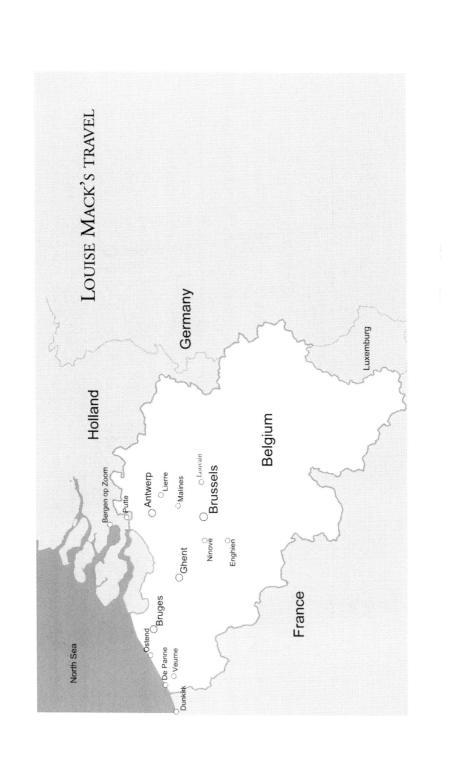

LOUISE MACK'S TRAVEL

MY ADVENTURES IN THE WAR ZONE.

(By Louise Mack, in "Answers.")

It is half-past one in the middle of the day. At least, people say it is half-past one. But the great gold clock over the Antwerp Cathedral has stopped since the day before, and its hands are still pointing mockingly to eight forty-five.

And now, through the livid sunless silences of the deserted city of Antwerp, which is still reeking horribly of powder, shrapnel, smoke, and burning petroleum, the Germans are coming down the Avenue de Commerce, to enter into possession of the surrendered city.

Suddenly I see a brown, lidded baker's cart dashing across the road at a desperate rate, wheeled by a poor old Belgian woman whose face is so wild, so hollow, that I whisper involuntarily as she passes me "Is there somebody ill inside your cart, madam?"

Without stopping, without looking even, her haggard eyes full of despair, the old woman mutters hoarsely:

"It's a dead soldier I have here, and he was my only son!"

She hurries on, almost at a run, to find a spot where she can bury her beloved dead before the Germans are all over the city.

And then I meet with my own first personal experience of the meaning of "German brute."

A young officer has espied a notice-board high up above a cafe on the left. A de-

ARE MEN BRAVER THAN WOMEN?

EXPERIENCES OF MISS LOUISE MACK.

IN ANTWERP DURING THE BOMBARDMENT.

Miss Louise Mack (Mrs. J. P. Creed) who arrived at the Outer Harbor by the Malwa yesterday, as might be expected, takes some pride in the fact that she was the last British war correspondent in Antwerp when that city fell to the Germans, but she speaks of her remarkable adventures in that doomed city and in other parts of Belgium after the occupation by the Teuton despoilers as if they were but incidents in a not unusually eventful career. Readers scarcely need be reminded that Miss Mack is an Australian authoress and journalist of note. "An Australian Girl in London" has introduced her to the people of her own country. Before the war so closely occupied her attention she wrote many novels, stories, and poems, but it is no reflection upon her former undoubtedly brilliant writings to say that her work as war correspondent in Antwerp for the London "Evening News" has made her fame greater even than did her novels and stories in times of peace. Miss Mack is a sister of Dr. Hans H. Mack, B.A., who many years ago was for some time a member of the literary staff of "The Advertiser." He graduated B.A. at the University of Adelaide, and afterwards took his medical degree in London. Miss Mack was born in Tasmania, and spent her early life in Australia. About 15 years ago she went to England. She has been absent from the Commonwealth since then, and now she is returning to see her people and the much loved home of her girlhood in Victoria. Into the last few months of her absence have been crowded more exciting events probably than have occurred in the lifetime of most other women. Her smiling, youthful face bears no trace of the awful things she has witnessed, and her spirit has not been quelled by her nerve-racking

LOUISE MACK.
WILL TELL WONDERFUL WAR STORIES.

Louise Mack, who shortly commences a series of war lectures in Australia, is of an adventurous disposition, and has had some thrilling encounters with the German military authorities while looking for "copy" as a journalist in Belgium. She tells of an extraordinary experience which she had while making Antwerp to Brussels. During her journey trains and even on the last stage from was of a timid party beaten wagonette driver. The roads far with the blue uniform and the conveyance quently in response to warning. "Les Allemaing down a road, how pany of Landsturm th a party of infantry Mack began to trembl a hoarse German di She felt that she was a suspected spy, but the other passengers darkest part of the red events. By a cars overlooked her papers on the screen during my lectures, because my story is such an extraordinary one that it seemed to me to be a wise thing than to authenticate it." An extraordinary story it is, indeed, but the most remarkable thing about it is that Miss Mack has sufficient self-control and serve to be able to recall and recount her adventures without breaking down. Most women, if they could have lived through it, would surely have been nervous wrecks. There were weeks of bombardment by Zeppelins or heavy guns, nerve-shattering concussions, and an everpresent menace of instant death. But the talks of her visit to Antwerp and the battlefields of Belgium as if it were but a morning parade in Hyde Park of which she spoke. Her chief impression upon reaching beleaguered Antwerp was of a beautiful city, with flowering in bloom, and red, black, and gold hanging from every house window; many would see the flowers upon trees where the sky was raining but. But this uncommon woman seems have had no knowledge of fear. "I King Albert several times," she said. in a magnificent looking man, but he more severe than the photographs would suggest. The Q is petite and loves to speak English. King is absolutely adored by he I saw two wounded soldiers walkin Antwerp after the bombardment, the by the arm and helped them a and I went into the hotel to get bread and cheese. They were tryin get out of the city I asked 'Where is your King?' You should see the look that came into his fac he replied. 'Vraiment, madame, je nais pas, mais je suis bien que 'Roi est sur le champs de bataille' don't know exactly where he is. know this, that he is on the field '!"

You speak of the beauties of Antw Was there no jarring note?

"It was tremendously crowded with refugees—people who had fled from to town before the Germans. Ant seemed to be the hope of Belgium no one had the slightest idea it ever fall."

Did you not find the bombard

LOUISE MACK.
FAMOUS WOMAN JOURNALIST.
Returns to Australia.

EXCITING WAR EXPERIENCES.

IN STRICKEN BELGIUM.

Mrs. Creed, known to the literary world as Louise Mack, an authoress and a famous war correspondent, returned to Australia to-day per the R.M.S. Malwa.

She is a native of Tasmania, but for 15 years. Mrs. Creed has already done a great deal of work in connection with the present great war. She the London "Evening the "Daily Mail" at the front. When she finally the latter city she refrom the London "Times" ber on the fact that est war correspondent to

WON INTERVIEW.

has long been an interous people, and she has the hardest-won interever came the way of This was with Monthe Burgomaster of Brussels will be remembered, was a German fortress for Germans all the money

AWFUL SACRILEGE AT AERSCHOTT.

Cathedral Strewn With Bottles and Filth.

HIGH ALTAR DESECRATED.

Head of Madonna Slashed Off and Crucifix Burnt.

Miss Louise Mack, of Sydney, Graphically Recounts Horrors.

LONDON, Wednesday.

Miss Louise Mack, a well-known journalist and verse writer of Sydney, who is now the Antwerp correspondent of the London "Evening News," has supplied a graphic narrative of the horrors which attended the German occupation of Aerschott, 9 miles north of Louvain.

After the Germans had departed a visit to the local cathedral showed that the edifice had been made the scene of festivity by the Germans. Many empty wine and beer bottles were found on the high altar, while in the confessionals were numbers of champagne and brandy bottles. The offertory box was stolen and replaced by a beer bottle. Bottles were stuck in

A WOMAN'S EXPERIENCES
IN THE GREAT WAR

CHAPTER I

CROSSING THE CHANNEL

"What do you do for mines?"

I put the question to the dear old salt at Folkestone quay, as I am waiting to go on board the boat for Belgium, this burning August night.

The dear old salt thinks hard for an answer, very hard indeed.

Then he scratches his head.

"There ain't none!" he makes reply.

All the same, in spite of the dear old salt, I feel rather creepy as the boat starts off that hot summer night, and through the pitch-black darkness we begin to plough our way to Ostend.

Over the dark waters the old English battleships send their vivid flashes unceasingly, but it is not a comfortable feeling to think you may be blown up at any minute, and I spend the hours on deck.

I notice our little fair-bearded Belgian captain is looking very sad and dejected.

"They're saying in Belgium now that our poor soldiers are getting all the brunt of it," he says despondently to a group of sympathetic war-correspondents gathered round him on deck, chattering, and trying to pick up bits of news.

"But that will all be made up," says Mr. Martin Donohue, the Australian War-Correspondent, who is among the crowd. "All that you lose will be given back to Belgium before long."

"*But they cannot give us back our dead,*" the little captain answers dully.

CHAPTER I

CROSSING THE CHANNEL

"What do you do for mines?"

I put the question to the dear old salt at Folkestone quay, as I am waiting to go on board the boat for Belgium, this burning August night.

The dear old salt thinks hard for an answer, very hard indeed.

Then he scratches his head.

"There ain't none!" he makes reply.

All the same, in spite of the dear old salt, I feel rather creepy as the boat starts off that hot summer night, and through the pitch-black darkness we begin to plough our way to Ostend.

Over the dark waters the old English battleships send their vivid flashes unceasingly, but it is not a comfortable feeling to think you may be blown up at any minute, and I spend the hours on deck.

I notice our little fair-bearded Belgian captain is looking very sad and dejected.

"They're saying in Belgium now that our poor soldiers are getting all the brunt of it," he says despondently to a group of sympathetic war-correspondents gathered round him on deck, chattering, and trying to pick up bits of news.

"But that will all be made up," says Mr. Martin Donohue, the Australian War-Correspondent, who is among the crowd. "All that you lose will be given back to Belgium before long."

"*But they cannot give us back our dead,*" the little captain answers dully.

And no one makes reply to that.

There is no reply to make.

It is four o'clock in the morning, instead of nine at night, when we get to Ostend at last, and the first red gleams of sunrise are already flashing in the east.

We leave the boat, cross the Customs, and, after much ringing, wake up the Belgian page-boy at the Hotel. In we troop, two English nurses, twenty War-Correspondents, and an "Australian Girl in Belgium." [1]

Rooms are distributed to us, great white lofty rooms with private bathrooms attached, very magnificent indeed.

Then, for a few hours we sleep, to be awakened by a gorgeous morning, golden and glittering, that shews the sea a lovely blue, but a very sad deserted town.

Poor Ostend!

Once she had been the very gayest of birds; but now her feathers are stripped, she is bare and shivery. Her big, white, beautiful hotels have dark blinds over all their windows. Her long line of blank, closed fronts of houses and hotels seems to go on for miles. Just here and there one is open. But for the most, everything is dead; and indeed, it is almost impossible to recognise in this haunted place the most brilliant seaside city in Europe.

It is only half-past seven; but all Ostend seems up and about as I enter the big salon and order coffee and rolls.

Suddenly a noise is heard, — shouts, wheels, something indescribable.

Everyone jumps up and runs down the long white restaurant.

Out on the station we run, and just then a motor dashes past us, coming right inside, under the station roof.

It is full of men.

And one is wounded.

My blood turns suddenly cold. I have never seen a wounded sol-

---

[1] This is a pun on Mack's novel *An Australian Girl in London* (1902).

dier before. I remember quite well I said to myself, "Then it is true. I had never really believed before!"

Now they are lifting him out, oh, so tenderly, these four other big, burly Belgians, and they have laid him on a stretcher.

He lies there on his back. His face is quite red. He has a bald head. He doesn't look a bit like my idea of a wounded soldier, and his expression remains unchanged. It is still the quiet, stolid, patient Belgian look that one sees in scores, in hundreds, all around.

And now they are carrying him tenderly on to the Red Cross ship drawn up at the station pier, and after a while we all go back and try and finish our coffee.

Barely have we sat down again before more shouts are heard.

Immediately, everybody is up and out on to the station, and another motor-car, full of soldiers, comes dashing in under the great glassed roofs.

Excitement rises to fever heat now.

Out of the car is dragged a *German*. And one can never forget one's first German. Never shall I forget that wounded Uhlan! One of his hands is shot off, his face is black with smoke and dirt and powder, across his cheek is a dark, heavy mark where a Belgian had struck him for trying to throttle one of his captors in the car.

He is a wretch, a brute. He has been caught with the Red Cross on one arm, and a revolver in one pocket. But there is yet something cruelly magnificent about the fellow, as he puts on that tremendous swagger, and marches down the long platform between two lines of foes to meet his fate.

As he passes very close to me, I look right into his face, and it is imprinted on my memory for all time.

He is a big, typical Uhlan, with round close-cropped head, blue eyes, arrogant lips, large ears, big and heavy of build. But what impresses me is that he is no coward.

He knows his destiny. He will be shot for a certainty – shot for wearing the Red Cross while carrying weapons. But he really is a splendid devil as he goes strutting down the long platform between the gendarmes, all alone among his enemies, alone in the last moments of his life. Then a door opens. He passes in. The door shuts. He will be seen no more!

All is panic now. We know the truth. The Germans have made a sudden sortie, and are attacking just at the edge of Ostend.

The gendarmes are fighting them, and are keeping them back.

Then a boy scout rushes in on a motor cycle, and asks for the Red Cross to be sent out at once; and then and there it musters in the dining-room of the Hotel, and rushes off in motor cars to the scene of action.

Then another car dashes in with another Uhlan, who has been shot in the back.

And now I watch the Belgians lifting their enemy out. All look of fight goes out of their faces, as they raise him just as gently, just as tenderly as they have raised their own wounded man a few moments ago, and carry him on to their Red Cross ship, just as carefully and pitifully.

"Quick! Quick!" A War-Correspondent hastens up. "There's not a minute to lose. The Kaiser has given orders that all English War-Correspondents will be shot on sight. The Germans will be here any minute. They will cut the telegraph wires, stop the boats, and shoot everyone connected with a newspaper."

The prospect finally drives us, with a panic-stricken crowd, on to the boat. And so, exactly six hours after we landed, we rush back again to England. Among the crowd are Italians, Belgians, British and a couple of Americans. An old Franciscan priest sits down, and philosophically tucks into a hearty lunch. Belgian priests crouch about in attitudes of great depression.

Poor priests!

They know how the Germans treat priests in this well-named "Holy War!"

CHAPTER II

ON THE WAY TO ANTWERP

A couple of days afterward, however, feeling thoroughly ashamed of having fled, and knowing that Ostend was now reinforced by English Marines, I gathered my courage together once more, and returned to Belgium.

This time, so that I should not run away again so easily, I took with me a suit-case, and a couple of trunks.

These trunks contained clothes enough to last a summer and a winter, the MS. of a novel – "Our Marriage," which had appeared serially, and all my chiffons.

In fact I took everything I had in my wardrobe. I thought it was the simplest thing to do. So it was. But it afterwards proved an equally simple way of losing all I had.

Getting back to Ostend, I left my luggage at the Maritime Hotel, and hurried to the railway station.

I had determined to go to Antwerp for the day and see if it would be possible to make my headquarters in that town.

"Pas de train!" said the ticket official.

"But why?"

"C'est la guerre!"

"Comment!"

"*C'est la guerre, Madame!*"

That was the answer one received to all one's queries in those days.

If you asked why the post had not come, or why the boat did not sail for England, or why your coffee was cold, or why your boots were not cleaned, or why your window was shut, or why the canary didn't sing, – you would always be sure to be told. "c'est la guerre!"

Next morning, however, the train condescended to start, and three hours after its proper time we steamed away from Ostend.

Slowly, painfully, through the hot summer day. our long, brown train went creeping towards Anvers!

Anvers!

The very name had grown into an emblem of hope in those sad days, when the Belgians were fleeing for their lives towards the safety of their great fortified city on the Scheldt.

Oh, to see them at every station, crushing in! In they crowd, and in they crowd, herding like dumb, driven cattle; and always the poor, white faced women with their wide, innocent eyes, had babies in their arms, and little fair-haired Flemish children hanging to their skirts. Wherever we stopped, we found the platforms lined ten deep and by the wildness with which these fugitive fought their way into the crowded carriages, one guessed at the pent-up terror in those poor hearts They *must*, they *must* get into that train! You could see it was a matter of life and death with them. And soon every compartment was packed, and on we went through the stifling, blinding August day – onwards towards Antwerp.

But when a soldier came along, how eager everyone was to find a place for him! Not one of us but would gladly give up our seat to any *soldat!* We would lean from the windows, and shout out loudly, almost imploringly, "Here, soldat! *Here!*" And when two wounded men from Malines appeared, we performed absolute miracles of compression in that long, brown train. We squeezed ourselves to nothing, we stood in back rows on the seats, while front rows sat on our toes, and the passage between the seats was packed so closely that one could scarcely insert a pin, and still we squeezed ourselves, and still fresh passengers came clambering in, and so wonderful was the spirit of goodwill abroad in these desperate days in Belgium, that we kept on making room for them, even when there was absolutely no more room to make!

Then a soldier began talking, and how we listened.

Never did priest, or orator, get such a hearing as that little blue-coated Belgian, white with dust, clotted with blood and mud, his yellow beard weeks old on his young face, with his poor feet in their broken boots, the original blue and red of his coat blackened with smoke, and hardened with earth where he had slept among the beetroots and potatoes at Malines.

He told us in a faint voice: "I often saw King Albert when I was fighting near Malines. Yes, he was there, our King! He was fighting too, I saw him many times, I was quite near him. Ah, he has a bravery and magnificence about him! I saw a shell exploding just a bare yard from where he was. Over and over again I saw his face, always calm and resolute. I hope all is well with him," he ended falteringly, "but in battle one knows nothing!"

"Yes, yes, all is well," answered a dozen voices. "King Albert is back at Antwerp, and safe with the Queen!"

A look of radiant happiness flashed over the poor fellow's face as he heard that.

Then he made us all laugh.

He said: "For two days I slept out in the fields, at first among the potatoes and the beetroots. And then I came to the asparagus." He drew himself up a bit. "*Savez vous?* The asparagus of Malines! It is the best asparagus in the world? *C'est ça! I AND I SLEPT ON IT, ON THE MALINES ASPARAGUS!*"

About noon that day we had arrived close to Ghent, when suddenly the train came to a standstill, and we were ordered to get out and told to wait on the platform.

"Two hours to wait!" the station-master told us.

The grey old city of Ghent, calm and massive among her monuments, looked as though war were a hundred miles away. The shops were all open. Business was being briskly done. Ladies were buying gloves and ribbons, old wide-bearded gentlemen were smoking their big cigars. Here and there was a Belgian officer. The shops were full of English papers.

I went into the Cathedral. It was Saturday morning, but great crowds of people, peasants, bourgeoisie and aristocracy, were there praying and telling their rosaries, and as I entered, a priest was finishing his sermon.

"Remember this, my children, remember this," said the little priest. "Only silence is great, the rest is weakness!"

It has often seemed to me since that those words hold the key-note to the Belgian character.

"*Seul la silence est grande; la teste est faiblesse.*"

For never does one hear a Belgian complain!

At last, over the flat, green country, came a glimpse of Antwerp, a great city lying stretched out on the flat lands that border the river Scheldt.

From the train-windows one saw a bewildering mass of taxi-cabs all gathered together in the middle of the green fields at the city's outskirts, for all the taxi-cabs had been commandeered by the Government. And near them was a field covered with monoplanes and biplanes, a magnificent array of aircraft of every kind, with the sunlight glittering over them like silver; they were all ready there to chase the Zeppelin when it came over from Cologne, and in the airfield a ceaseless activity went on.

Slowly and painfully our train crept into Antwerp station. The pomp and spaciousness of this building, with its immense dome-like roof, was very striking. It was the second largest station in the world. And in those days it had need to be large, for the crowds that poured out of the trains were appalling. All the world seemed to be rushing into the fortified town. Soldiers were everywhere, and for the first time I saw men armed to the teeth, with bayonets drawn, looking stern and implacable, and I soon found it was a very terrible affair to get inside the city. I had to wait and wait in a dense crowd for quite an hour before I could get to the first line of sentinels. Then I shewed my passport and papers, while two Belgian sentinels stood on each side of me, their bayonets horribly near my head.

Out in the flagged square I got a fiacre, and started off for a drive.

My first impression of Antwerp, as I drove through it that golden day, was something never, never to be forgotten.

As long as I live I shall see that great city, walled in all round with magnificent fortifications, standing ready for the siege. Along the curbstones armed guards were stationed, bayonets fixed, while dense crowds seethed up and down continually. In the golden sunlight thousands of banners were floating in the wind, enormous banners of a size such as I had never seen before, hanging out of these great, white stately houses along the avenues lined with acacias. There were banners fluttering out of the shops along the Chaussee de Malines, banners floating from the beautiful cathedral, banners, banners, everywhere. Hour after hour I drove, and everywhere there were banners, golden, red and black, floating on the breeze. It seemed to me that that black struck a curiously sombre note – almost a note of warning, and I confess that I did not quite like it, and I even thought to myself that if I were a Belgian, I would raise heaven and earth to have the black taken out of my national flag. Alas, one little dreamed, that golden summer day, of the tragic fate that lay in wait for Antwerp! In those days we all believed her utterly impregnable.

After a long drive, I drove to the Hotel Terminus to get a cup of tea and arrange for my stay.

It gave me a feeling of surprise to walk into a beautiful, palm-lined corridor, and see people sitting about drinking cool drinks and eating ices. There were high-spirited dauntless Belgian officers, in their picturesque uniforms, French and English business men, and a sprinkling of French and English War-Correspondents. A tall, charming grey-haired American lady with the Red Cross on her black chiffon sleeve was having tea with her husband, a grey-moustached American Army Doctor. These were Major and Mrs. Livingstone Seaman, a wealthy philanthropic American couple, who were devoting their lives and their substance to helping Red Cross work.

Suddenly a man came towards me.

"You don't remember me," he said. "You are from Australia! I met you fifteen years ago in Sydney."

It was a strange meeting that, of two Australians, who were destined later on to face such terrific odds in that city on the Scheldt.

"My orders are," Mr. Frank Fox told me as we chatted away, "to stick it out. Whatever happens, I've got to see it through for the *Morning Post.*"

"And I'm going to see it through, too," I said.

"Oh no!" said Mr. Fox. "You'll have to go as soon as trouble threatens!"

"Shall I?" I thought.

But as he was a man and an Australian, I did not think it was worth while arguing the matter with him. Instead, we talked of Sydney, and old friends across the seas, the Blue mountains, and the Bush,[2] and our poets and writers and painters and politicians, friends of long ago, forgetting for the moment that we were chatting as it were on the edge of a crater.

---

[2] In Australia "bush" refers to any region outside of the major metropolitan areas, so generally to the typical Australian landscape. The term is iconic and often seen as national symbol.

CHAPTER III

GERMANS ON THE LINE

I was coming back with my luggage from Ostend next day when the train, which had been running along at a beautiful speed, came to a standstill somewhere near Bruges.

There was a long wait, and at last it became evident that something was wrong.

A brilliant-looking Belgian General, accompanied by an equally brilliant Belgian Captain, who had travelled up in the train with me from Ostend, informed me courteously, that it was doubtful if the train would go on to-day.

"What has happened?" I asked.

"Les Allemands sont sur la ligne!" was the graphic answer.

With the Belgians' courteous assistance, I got down my suit-case, arid a large brown paper parcel, for of course in those day, no one thought anything of a brown paper parcel; in fact it was quite the correct thing to be seen carrying one, no matter who you were, king, queen, general, prince, or war-correspondent.

"Do you see that station over there?" Le Capitaine said. "Well, in a few hours' time, a train *may* start from there, and run to Antwerp but it will not arrive at the ordinary station. It will go as far as the river, and then we shall get on board a steamer, and cross the river, and shall arrive at Antwerp from the quay."

Picking up my suit-case he started off, with the old General beside him carrying my parasols, while I held my brown paper parcel firmly under one arm, and grasped my hand-bag with the other hand. I was just thinking to myself how nice it was to have a General and a Capitaine looking after me, when, to my supreme disgust, my brown paper parcel burst open, and there fell out an evening shoe. And such a shoe! It was a brilliant blue and equally brilliant silver, with a very high heel, and a big silver buckle. It was a shoe I loved, and I hadn't felt like leaving it behind. And now there it fell on the station, witness to a woman's vanity. However, the Belgian Captain was quite equal to the occasion. He picked it up, and presented it to me with a bow, and said, in unexpected English, "Yourra Sabbath shoe!"

It was good to have little incidents like that to brighten one's journey, for a very long and tedious time elapsed before we arrived at Antwerp that night. The crowded, suffocating train crawled along, and stopped half an hour indiscriminately every now and then, and we wondered if the Germans were out there in the flat fields to either side of us.

When we arrived at the Scheldt, I trudged wearily on to the big river steamboat, more dead than alive. The General was still carrying my parasols, and the Capitaine still clung to my suit-case, and at last we crossed the great blue Scheldt, and landed on the other side, where a row of armed sentinels presented their bayonets at us, and kept us a whole hour examining our passports before they would allow us to enter the city.

Thanks to the kindly General, I got a lift in a motor-car, and was taken straight to the Hotel Terminus. I had eaten nothing since the morning. But the sleepy hotel night-porter told me it was impossible to get anything at that hour; everything was locked up; *"C'est la guerre!"* he said.

Well, he was right; it was indeed the War, and I didn't feel that I had any call to complain or make a fuss, so I wearily took the lift up to my bedroom on the fourth floor, and speedily fell asleep.

When I awoke, *it was three o'clock in the morning*, and a most terrific noise was going on.

It was pitch dark, darker than any words can say, up there in my bedroom, for we were forbidden lights for fear of Zeppelins.

All day long I had been travelling through Belgium, and all day long, it seemed to me, I had been turned out of one train into another, because "les Allemands" were on the line.

So, when the noise awoke me, I knew at once it was those Germans that I had been running away from all day long, between Ostend and Bruges, and Bruges and Ghent, and Ghent and Boom, and Antwerp.

I lay quite still.

"They're come at last," I thought. "This is the real thing."

Vaguely I wondered what to do.

The roar of cannon was enormous, and it seemed to be just outside my window.

And cracking and rapping through it, I heard the quick, incessant fire of musketry – crack, crack, crack, a beautiful, clean noise, like millions of forest boughs sharply breaking in strong men's hands.

Vaguely I listened.

And vaguely I tried to imagine how the Germans could have got inside Antwerp so quickly.

Then vaguely I got out of bed.

In the pitch blackness, so hot and stifling, I stood there trying to think, but my room seemed full of the roar of cannon, and I experienced a queer sensation as though I was losing consciousness in the sea, under the loud beat of waves.

"I mustn't turn up the light," I said to myself, "or they will see where I am! That's the *one* thing I mustn't do."

Again I tried to think what to do, and then suddenly I found myself listening, with a subconsciousness of immense and utter content, to the wild outcry of those cannons and muskets, and I felt as if I must listen, and listen, and listen, till I knew the sounds by heart. As for fear, there was none, not any at all, not a particle.

Instead, there was something curiously akin to rapture.

It seemed to me that the supreme satisfaction of having at last dropped clean away from all the make-believes of life, seized upon me, standing there in my nightgown in the pitchblack, airless room at Antwerp, a woman quite alone among strangers, with danger knocking at the gate of her world.

Make-believe! Make-believe! All life up to this minute seemed nothing else but make-believe. For only Death seemed real, and only Death seemed glorious.

All this took me about two minutes to think, and then I began to move about my room, stupidly, vaguely.

I seemed to bump up against the noise of the cannons at every step. But I could not find the door, and I could not find a wrapper.

My hands went out into the darkness, grabbing, reaching.

But all the while I was listening with that deep, undisturbed content to the terrific fire that seemed to shake the earth and heaven to pieces.

All I could get hold of was the sheet and blankets.

I had arrived back at my bed again.

Well, I must turn away, I must look elsewhere.

And then I quietly and unexpectedly put out my hand and turned up the light in a fit of desperate defiance of the German brutes outside.

In a flash I saw my suit-case. It was locked. I saw my powder puff. I saw my bag. Then I put out the light and picked up my powder-puff, got to my bag, and fumbled for the keys, and opened my suit-case and dragged out a wrapper, but no slippers came under my fingers, and I wanted slippers in case of going out into the streets.

But by this time I had discovered that nothing matters at all, and I quietly turned up the light again, being by then a confirmed and age-old fatalist.

Standing in front of the looking-glass, I found myself slowly powdering my face.

Then the sound of people rushing along the corridor reached me, and I opened my door and went out.

"C'est une bataille! Ce sont les Allemands, n'est-ce-pas?" queried a poor old lady.

"Mais non, madame," shouts a dashing big aeronaut running by. "Ce n'est pas une bataille. C'est le Zeppelin!"

And so it was.

The Zeppelin had come, for the second time, to Antwerp! And the cannons and musketry were the onslaughts upon the monster by the Belgian soldiers, mad with rage at the impudent visit, and all ready with a hot reception for it.

Down the stairs I fled, snatched away now from those wonderful moments of reality, alone, with the noise of the cannons in the pitch-blackness of that Stirling bedroom; down the great scarlet-carpeted stairs, until we all came to a full stop in the hotel lounge below.

One dim light, shaded half into darkness, revealed the silhouettes of tall, motionless green palms and white wicker chairs and scarlet carpets and little tables, and the strangest crowd in all the world.

The Zeppelin was sailing overhead just then, flinging the ghastliest of all ghastly deaths from her cages as she sped along her craven way across the skies, but that crowd in the foyer of the great Antwerp Hotel remained absolutely silent, absolutely calm.

There was a tiny boy from Liege, whose trembling pink feet peeped from the blankets in which he had been carried down.

There was a lovely heroic Liege lady whose gaiety and sweetness, and charming toilettes had been making "sunshine in a shady place" for us all in these dark days.

Everyone remembered afterwards how beautiful the little Liege lady looked with her great, black eyes, still sparkling, and long red-black hair falling over her shoulders, and a black wrapper flung over her white nightgown.

And her husband, a huge, fair-haired Belgian giant with exquisite manners and a little-boy lisp – a daring aviator – never seen except in a remarkable pair of bright yellow bags of trousers. His lisp was unaffected, and his blue eyes bright and blue as spring flowers, and his heart was iron-strong.

And there was Madame la Patronne, wrapped in a good many things; and an Englishman with a brown moustache, who must have had an automatic toilette, as he is here fully dressed, even to his scarf-pin, hat, boots and all; and some War-Correspondents, who always

have the incontestable air of having arranged the War from beginning
to end, especially when they appear like this in their pyjamas; and a
crowd of Belgian ladies and children, and all the maids and garcons,
and the porters and the night-porters, and various strange old gentlemen in overcoats and bare legs, and strange old ladies with their
heads tied, who will never be seen again (not to be recognised), and
the cook from the lowest regions, and the chasseur who runs messages – there we all were, waiting while the Zeppelin sailed overhead,
and the terrific crash and boom and crack and deafening detonations
grew fainter and fainter as the Belgian soldiers fled along through the
night in pursuit of the German dastard that was finally driven back
to Cologne, having dashed many houses to bits.

Then the little "chass," who has run through the street-door away
down the road, comes racing back breathless across the flagged stone
court-yard.

"Oh, mais c'est chic, le Zepp," he cries enthusiastically, his young
black eyes afire. "C'est tout a fait chic, vous savez!"

And if that's not truly Beige, I really don't know what is!

CHAPTER IV

IN THE TRACK OF THE HUNS

When I look back on those days, the most pathetic thing about it all seems to me the absolute security in which we imagined ourselves dwelling.

The King and Queen were in their Palace, that tall simple flat-fronted grey house in the middle of the town. Often one saw the King, seated in an open motor car coming in and out of the town, or striding quickly into the Palace. Tall and fair, his appearance always seemed to me to undergo an extraordinary change from the face as shewn in photographs. It was because in real life those beautiful wide blue eyes of his, mirrors of truth and simple courage, were covered with glasses.

And "la petite Reine," equally beloved, was very often to be seen too, driving backwards and forwards to the hospitals, the only visits she ever paid.

All theatres were closed, all concerts, all cinemas. All the galleries were shut. Never a note of song or music was to be heard anywhere. To open a piano at one's hotel would have been a crime.

And yet, that immense crowd gathered together in Antwerp for safety, Ambassadors, Ministers and their wives and families, Consuls, Echevins, merchants, stockbrokers, peasants, were anything but gloomy. A peculiar tide of life flowed in and out through that vast cityful of people. It was life, vibrant with expectation, thrilling with hope and fear, without a moment's loneliness. They walked about the shady avenues. They sat at their cafes, they talked, they sipped their coffee, or their "Elixir d'Anvers" and then they went home to bed. After seven the streets were empty, the cafes shut, the day's life ended.

Never a doubt crossed our minds that the Germans could possibly get through those endless fortifications surrounding Antwerp on all sides.

Getting about was incredibly difficult. In fact, without a car, one could see nothing, and there were no cars to be had, the War Office had taken them all over. In despair I went to Sir Frederick Greville, the English Ambassador, and after certain formalities and inquiries, Sir Frederick very kindly went himself to the War Office, saw Count Chabean on my behalf, and arranged for my getting a car.

Many a dewy morning, while the sun was low in the East, I have started out and driven along the road to Ghent, or to Liege, or to Malines, and looking from the car I observed those endless forests of wire, and the mined waters whose bridges one drove over so slowly, so softly, in such fear and trembling. And then, set deep in the great fortified hillsides, the mouths of innumerable cannon pointed at one; and here and there great reflectors were placed against the dull earth-works to shew when the enemy's air-craft appeared in the skies. Nothing seemed wanting to make those fortifications complete and successful. It was heart-breaking to see the magnificent old chateaux and the beautiful little houses being ruthlessly cut down, razed to the earth to make clear ground in all directions for the defence-works. The stumps of the trees used to look to me like the ruins of some ancient city, for even they represented the avenues of real streets and roads, and the black, empty places behind them were the homes that had been demolished in this overwhelming attempt to keep at least one city of Belgium safe and secure from the marauding Huns.

Afterwards, when all was over, when Antwerp had fallen, I passed through the fortifications for the last time on my way to Holland. And oh, the sadness of it! There were the wire entanglements, untouched, unaltered! The great reflectors still mirrored the sunlight and the stars. The demolition of the chateaux and house had been all in vain. On this side there had been little fighting, they had got in on the other side.

Every five minutes one's car would be held up by sentinels who rushed forward with poised bayonets, demanding the password for the day.

That always seemed to me like a bit of mediaeval history.

"Arretez!" cried the sentinels, on either side the road, lifting their rifles as they spoke.

Of course we came to a stop immediately.

Then the chauffeur would lean far out, and whisper in a hoarse, low voice, the password, which varied with an incessant variety. Sometimes it would be "Ostend" or "Termond" or "Demain" or "General" or "Bruxelles" or "Belgique" or whatever the War Office chose to make it. Then the sentinel would nod. "Good", he would say, and on we would go.

The motor car lent me by the Belgian War Office, was driven by an excitable old Belgian, who loved nothing better than to get into a dangerous spot. His favourite saying, when we got near shell-fire, and one asked him if he were frightened, was: "One can only die once." And the louder the shells, the quicker he drove towards them; and I used to love the way his old eyes flashed, and I loved too the keenly disappointed look that crept over his face when the sentinels refused to let him go any nearer the danger line, and we had to creep ignominiously back to safety.

"Does not your master ever go towards the fighting?" I asked him.

"Non, madame," he answered sadly, "Mon general, he is the PAPA of the Commissariat! He does not go near the fighting. He only looks after the eating."

We left Antwerp one morning about nine o'clock, and sped outwards through the fortifications, being stopped every ten minutes as usual by the sentinels and asked to show our papers. On we ran along the white tree-lined roads through exquisite green country. The roads were crowded constantly with soldiers coming and going, and in all the villages we found the Headquarters of one or other Division of the Belgian Army, making life and bustle indescribable in the flagged old streets, and around the steps of the quaint mediaeval Town Halls and Cathedrals.

We had gone a long way when we were brought to a standstill at a little place called Heyst-opden Berg, where the sentinels leaned into our car and had a long friendly chat with us.

"You cannot go any further," they said. "The Germans are in the next town ahead; they are only a few kilometres away."

"What town is it?" I asked.

"Aerschot," they replied.

"That is on the way to Lou vain, is it not?" I asked. "I have been trying for a long time to get to Louvain!"

"You can never get to Louvain, Madam," the sentinels told me smilingly. "Between here and Louvain lies the bulk of the German Army."

Just then, a *chasseur*, mounted on a beautiful fiery little brown Ardennes horse, came galloping along, shouting as he passed, "The Germans have been turned out of Aerschot; we have driven them out, *les sales cochons!* "

He jumped off his horse, gave the reins to a soldier and leapt into a train that was standing at the station.

A sudden inspiration flashed into my head. Without a word I jumped out of the motor car, ran through the station, and got into that train just as it was moving off, leaving my old Belgian to look after the car.

Next moment I found myself being carried along through unknown regions, and as I looked from the windows I soon discovered that I had entered now into the very heart of German ruin and pillage and destructiveness. Pangs of horror attacked me at the sight of those blackened roofless houses, standing lonely and deserted among green, thriving fields. I saw one little farm after another reduced to a heap of blackened ashes, with some lonely animals gazing terrifiedly into space. Sometimes just one wall would be standing of what was once a home, sometimes only the front of the house had been blown out by shells, and you could see right inside, — see the rooms spread out before you like a panorama, see the children's toys and frocks lying about, and the pots and pans, even the remains of dinner still on the table, and all the homely little things that made you feel so intensely the difference between this chill, deathly desolation and the happy domestic life that had gone on in such peaceful streams before the Huns set their faces Belgium-wards.

Mile after mile the train passed through these ravaged areas, and I stood at the window with misty eyes and quickened breath, looking up and down the lonely roads, and over the deserted fields where never a soul was to be seen, and in my mind's eye, I could follow those peasants, fleeing, fleeing, ever fleeing from one village to another, from one town to another, hunted and followed by the cruel menace of War which they, poor innocent ones, had done so little to deserve.

The only comfort was to think of them getting safely across to England, and as I looked at those little black and ruined homes, I could follow the refugees in their flight and see them streaming out of the trains at Victoria and Charing Cross, and being taken to warm, comfortable homes and clothed and fed by gentle-voiced English people. And then, waking perhaps in the depths of the night to find themselves in a strange land, how their thoughts would fly, with what awful yearning, back to those little blackened homes, back to the memories of the cow and the horse and the faithful dogs, and the corn in the meadows, and the purple cabbages uncut and the apples ungarnered! Yes, I could see it all, and my heart ached as it had never ached before.

When I roused myself from these sad thoughts, I looked about me and discovered that I was in a train full of nothing but soldiers and priests. I sat very still in my corner. I asked no questions, and spoke to no one. I knew by instinct that this train was going to take me to a place that I never should have arrived at otherwise, and I was right. The train took me to Aerschot, and I may say now that only one other War-Correspondent arrived there.

Alighting at the station at Aerschot, I looked about me, scarcely believing that what I saw was real.

The railway station appeared to have fallen victim to an earthquake.

CHAPTER V

AERSCHOT

I think until that day I had always cherished a lurking hope that the Huns were not as black as they were painted.

I had been used to think of the German race, as tinged with a certain golden glamour, because to it belonged the man who wrote the Fifth Symphony; the man who wrote the divine first part of "Faust," and still more that other, whose mocking but sublime laughter would be a fitting accompaniment of the horrors at Aerschot.

Oh, Beethoven, Goethe, Heine! Not even out of respect for your undying genius can I hide the truth about the Germans any longer.

What I have seen, I must believe!

In the pouring rain, wearing a Belgian officer's great-coat, I trudged along through a city that might well have been Pompeii or Herculaneum; it was a city that existed no longer; it was absolutely *the shell of a town*. The long streets were full of hollow, blackened skeletons of what had once been houses – street upon street of them, and street upon street. The brain reeled before the spectacle. And each of those houses once a home. A place of thought, of rest, of happiness, of work, of love.

All the inhabitants have fled, leaving their lares and penates just as the people of Pompeii and Herculaneum sought to flee when the lava came down on them.

Here a wall stands, there a pillar and a few bricks.

But between the ruins, strange, touching, unbelievable, gleaming from the background, are the scarlet and white of dahlias and roses in the gardens behind, that have somehow miraculously escaped the ruin that has fallen on the solid walls and ceilings and floors so carefully constructed by the brain of man, and so easily ruined by man's brutality.

It is as though the flowers had some miraculous power of self-preservation, some secret unknown to bricks and mortar, some strange magic, that keeps the sweet blossoms laughing and defiant under the Hun's shell-fire. And the red and the pure white of them, and the green, intensify, with a tremendous potency, the black horrors of the town!

In every street I observed always the same thing; hundreds of empty bottles. "Toujours *les bouteilles*" one of my companions kept saying – a brilliant young Brussels lawyer who was now in this regiment. The other officer was also a *Bruxellois*, and I was told afterwards that these two had formerly been the "Nuts" of Brussels, the two smartest young men of the town. To see them that day gave little idea of their smartness; they both were black with grime and smoke, with beards that had no right to be there, creeping over their faces, boots caked with mud to the knees, and a general air of having seen activities at very close quarters.

They took me to the church, and there the little old brown-faced sacristan joined us, punctuating our way with groans and sobs of horror.

This is what I see.

Before me stretches a great dim interior lit with little bunches of yellow candles. It is in a way a church. But what has happened to it? What horror has seized upon it, turning it into the most hideous travesty of a church that the world has ever known?

On the high altar stand empty champagne bottles, empty rum bottles, a broken bottle of Bordeaux, and five bottles of beer.

In the confessionals stand empty champagne bottles, empty brandy bottles, empty beer bottles.

In the Holy Water fonts are empty brandy bottles.

Stacks of bottles are under the pews, or on the seats themselves.

Beer, brandy, rum, champagne, bordeaux, burgundy; and again beer, brandy, rum, champagne, bordeaux, burgundy.

Everywhere, everywhere, in whatever part of the church one looks, there are bottles – hundreds of them, thousands of them, perhaps – everywhere, bottles, bottles, bottles.

The sacred marble floors are covered everywhere with piles of straw, and bottles, and heaps of refuse and filth, and horse-dung.

"Mais Madame," cries the burning, trembling voice of the distracted sacristan, "look at this."

And he leads me to the white marble bas-relief of the Madonna.

The Madonna's head has been cut right off!

Then, even as I stand there trying to believe that I am really looking at such nightmares, I feel the little sacristan's fingers trembling on my arm, turning me towards a sight that makes me cold with horror.

They have set fire to the Christ, to the beautiful wood-carving of our Saviour, and burnt the sacred figure all up one side, and on the face and breast.

And as they finished the work I can imagine them, with a hiccup slitting up the priceless brocade on the altar with a bayonet, then turning and slashing at the great old oil paintings on the Cathedral walls, chopping them right out of their frames, but leaving the empty frames there, with a German's sense of humour that will presently make Germany laugh on the wrong side of its face.

A dead pig lies in the little chapel to the right, a dead white pig with a pink snout.

Very still and pathetic is that dead pig, and yet it seems to speak.

It seems to realise the sacrilege of its presence here in God's House.

It seems to say, "Let not the name of pig be given to the Germans. We pigs have done nothing to deserve it."

"And here, Madame, voyez vous! Here the floor is chipped and smashed where they stabled their horses, these barbarians!" says the young Lieutenant on my left.

And now we come to the Gate of Shame.

It is the door of a small praying-room.

Still pinned outside, on the door, is a piece of white paper, with this message in German, "This room is private. Keep away."

And inside?

Inside are women's garments, a pile of them tossed hastily on the floor, torn perhaps from the wearers....

A pile of women's garments!

In silence we stand there. In silence we go out. It is a long time before anyone can speak again, though the little sacristan keeps on moaning to himself.

As we step out of the horrors of that church some German prisoners that have just been brought in, are being marched by.

And then rage overcomes one of the young Lieutenants. White, trembling, beside himself, he rushes forward. He shouts. He raves. He is thinking of that room; they were of Belgium, those girls and women; he is of Belgium too; and he flings his scorn and hatred at the Uhlans marching past, he lashes and whips them with his agony of rage until the cowering prisoners are out of hearing.

The other Lieutenant at last succeeds in silencing him.

"What is the use, mon ami!" he says. "What is the use?"

Perhaps this outburst is reported to headquarters by somebody. For that night at the Officers' Mess, the Captain of the regiment has a few words to say against shewing anger towards prisoners, and very gently and tactfully he says them.

He is a Belgian, and all Belgians are careful to a point that is almost beyond human comprehension in their criticisms of their enemies.

"Let us be careful never to demean ourselves by humiliating prisoners," says the Captain, looking round the long roughly-set table. "You see, my friends, these poor German fellows that we take are not all typical of the crimes that the Germans commit; lots of them are only peasants, or men that would prefer to stay by their own fireside!"

"What about Aerschot and the church?" cry a score of irritated young voices.

The Captain draws his kindly lips together, and attacks his black bread and tinned mackerel.

"Ah," he says, "we must remember they were all drunk!"
And as he utters these words there flash across my mind those old, old words that will never die:
"Forgive them, for they know not what they do."

CHAPTER VI

THE SWIFT RETRIBUTION

As I stood in the rain, down there in the ruined blackened piazza of Aerschot, someone drew my attention to the hole in the back-window of the Burgomaster's house.

In cold blood, the Germans had shot the Burgomaster.

And they had shot two of his children.

And as they could not find the Burgomaster's wife, who had fled into the country, they had offered 4,000 francs reward for her.

A hoarse voice whispered that in that room with the broken window, the German Colonel who had ordered the murder of the good, kind, beloved Burgomaster, had met his own fate.

Yes! In the room of the dead Burgomaster's maidservant, the German colonel had fallen dead from a shot fired from without.

By whose hand was it fired, that shot that laid the monster at his victim's feet?

"By the hand of an inferieur!" someone whispers.

And I put together the story, and understand that the girl's village sweetheart avenged her. They are both dead now – the girl and her village swain – shot down instantly by the howling Germans.

But their memory will never die; for they stand – that martyred boy and girl, – for Belgium's fight for its women's honour and the manliness of its men.

CHAPTER VII

THEY WOULD NOT KILL THE COOK

Besides myself, I discover only one woman in the whole of Aerschot — a little fair-haired Fleming, with a lion's heart. She is the bravest woman in the world. I love the delightful way she drops her wee six-weeks-old baby into my arms, and goes off to serve a hundred hungry Belgians with black bread and coffee, confident that her little treasure will be quite safe in the lap of the "Anglaise."

Smiling and running about between the kitchen, the officers' mess, and the bar, this brave, good soul finds time to tell us how she remained all alone in Aerschot for three whole weeks, all the while the Germans were in possession of the town.

"I knew that cooking they must have," she says, "and food and drink, and for that I knew I was safe. So I remained here, and kept the hotel of my little husband from being burned to the ground! But I slept always with my baby in my arms, and the revolver beside the pillow. In the night sometimes I heard them knocking at my door. Yes, they would knock, knock, knock! And I would lie there, the revolver ready, if needs be, for myself and the petite both! But they never forced that door. They would go away as stealthily as they had come! Ah! they knew that if they had got in they would have found a dead woman, not a live one!"

And I quite believed her.

CHAPTER VIII

"YOU'LL NEVER GET THERE"

As the weeks went on a strange thing happened to me.

At first vaguely, faintly, and then with an ever-deepening intensity, there sprang to life within me a sense of irritation at having to depend on newspapers, or hearsay, for one's knowledge of the chief item in this War, – the Enemy.

An overwhelming desire seized upon me to discover for myself what a certain darksome unknown quantity was like; that darksome, unknown quantity that we were always hearing about but never saw; that we were always moving away from if we heard it was anywhere near; that was making all the difference to everything; that was at the back of everything; that mattered so tremendously; and yet could never be visualized.

The habit of a life-time of groping for realities began to assert itself, and I found myself chafing at not being able to find things out for myself.

In the descriptions I gleaned from men and newspapers I was gradually discovering many puzzling incongruities.

There are thinkers whose conclusions one honours, and attends to: but these thinkers were not out here, looking at the War with their own eyes. Maeterlinck, for instance, whose deductions would have been invaluable, was in France. Tolstoi was dead. Mr. Wells was in England writing.[3]

---

[3] They are Maurice Maeterlinck (1862-1949), Belgian writer that awarded Nobel Prize in

To believe what people tell you, you must first believe in the people. If you can find one person to believe in in a lifetime, and that one person is yourself, you are lucky!

One day, towards the end of September, I heard an old professor from Liége University talking to a young Bruxellois with a black moustache and piercing black eyes, who had arrived that day at our hotel.

"So you are going back at once to Brussels, Monsieur?" said the old professor in his shaky voice.

"Yes, Monsieur! Why don't you come with me?"

"I have not the courage!"

"Courage! But there is nothing to fear! You come along with me, and I'll see you through all right. I assure you the trains run right into Brussels now. The Germans leave us Bruxellois alone. They're trying to win our favour. They never interfere with us. There is not the slightest danger. And there is not half so much trouble and difficulty to get in and out of Brussels as there is to get in and out Antwerp. You get into a train at Ghent, go to Grammont, and there chang into a little train that takes you straight to Brussels They never ask us for our passports now. For myself, I have come backwards and forwards from Brussels half a dozen times this last fortnight on special missions for our Government. I have never been stopped once. If you'll trust yourself to me, I'll see you safely through!"

"I desire to go very much!" muttered the old man. "There are things in Liége that I must attend to. But to get to Liége I must go through Brussels. It seems to me there is a great risk, a very great risk."

"No risk at all!" said the young Bruxellois cheerfully.

That evening at dinner, the young man aforesaid was introduced to me by Mr. Frank Fox of the *Morning Post*, who knew him well.

It was not long before I said to him: "Do you think it would be possible for an Englishwoman to get into Brussels? I should like very

Literature in 1911, and lived in France at that time; Lev Tolstoj, dead in 1910; Herbet George Wells (1866-1946).

much to go. I want to get an interview with M. Max for my newspaper." [4]

He was an extremely optimistic and cheerful young man.

He said, "Quite easy! I know M. Max very well. If you come with me, I'll see you safely through, and take you to see him. As a matter of fact I've got a little party travelling with me on Friday, and I shall be delighted if you will join us."

"I'll come," I said.

Extraordinary how easy it is to make up one's mind about big things.

That decision, which was the most important one I ever made in my life, gave me less trouble than I have sometimes been caused by such trifles as how to do one's hair or what frock to wear.

Next day, I told everyone I was going to try to get into Brussels.

"You'll be taken prisoner!"

"You're mad!"

"You'll be shot!"

"You will be taken for a spy!"

"You will never get there!"

All these things, and hosts of others, were said, but perhaps the most potent of all the arguments was that put up by the sweet little lady from Liége, the black-eyed mother with two adorable little boys, and a delightful big husband – the gallant chevalier, in yellow bags of trousers, whom I have already referred to in an earlier chapter.

This little Liégoise and I were now great friends; I shall speak of her as Alice. She had a gaiety and insouciance, and a natural childlike merriment that all her terrible disasters could not overcloud. What laughs we used to have together, she and I, what talks, what walks! And sometimes the big husband would give Alice a delightful little dinner at the Criterium Restaurant in the Avenue de Kaiser, where

[4] Adolphe Max (1869-1939) was Mayor of Brussels at the time of German invasion. He was popular for refusing to cooperate with the occupying forces, so that he was held in captivity until the end of the war.

we ate such delicious things, it was impossible to believe oneself in a Belgian city with War going on at the gates.

When I told Alice that I was going to Brussels she set to work with all her womanly powers of persuasion to make me give up my project.

There was nothing she did not urge.

The worst of all was that we might never see each other again.

"But I don't feel like that," I told her. "I feel that I must go! It's a funny feeling, I can't describe it, because it isn't exactly real. I don't feel exactly that I must go. Even when I am telling you that, it isn't exactly true."

"I am afraid this is too complicated for me," said Alice gravely.

"I admit it sounds complicated! I suppose what it really mean is that I want to go, and I am going!"

"But my husband says we may be in Brussels ourselves in three weeks' time: why not wait and come in in safety with the Belgian Army!"

Other people gathered round us, there in the dimly-lit palm court of the big Antwerp Hotel, and a lively discussion went on.

A big dark man, with a melancholy face, said wistfully, "I wish I could make up my mind to go too!"

This was Cherry Kearton, the famous naturalist and photographer.[5] He was out at the front looking for pictures, and in his mind's eye, doubtless, he saw the pictures he would get in Brussels, pictures sneakingly and stealthily taken from windows at the risk of one's life, glorious pictures, pictures a photographer would naturally see in his mind's eye when he thought of getting into Brussels during the German occupation.

Mr. Kearton's interpreter, a little fair-haired man, however, put in a couple of sharp words that were intended to act as an antidote to the great photographer's uncertain longings.

---

[5] Cherry Kearton (1871-1940), was one of the world's earliest wildlife photographers and writers.

"You'll be shot for a dead certainty, Cherry?" he said. "You get into Brussels with your photographic apparatus! Why, you might as well walk straight out to the Germans and ask them to finish you off!"

"Cherry" had his old enemy, malaria, hanging about him at that time, or I quite believe he would have risked it and come.

But as events turned out it was lucky for him he didn't! For his King and his Country have called him since then in a voice he could not resist, and he has gone to his beloved Africa again, in Colonel Driscoll's League of Frontiersmen.

When I met him out there in Antwerp, he had just returned from his famous journey across Central Africa. His thoughts were all of lions, giraffes, monkeys, rhinoceros. He would talk on and on, quite carried away. He made noises like baboons, boars, lions, monkeys. He was great fun. I was always listening to him, and gradually I would forget the War, forget I was in Antwerp, and be carried right away into the jungle watching a crowd of giraffes coming down to drink.

Indeed the vividness of Cherry's stories was such, that, when I think of Antwerp now, I hear the roar of lions, the pad pad of wild beasts, the gutteral uncouthness of monkeys – all the sounds in fact that so excellently represent Antwerp's present occupiers! But the faces of Cherry's wild beasts were kinder, humaner faces than the faces that haunt Antwerp now.

CHAPTER IX

SETTING OUT ON THE GREAT ADVENTURE

It was on Friday afternoon, September 24th, that I ran down the stairs of the Hotel Terminus, with a little brown bag in my hand.

Without saying good-bye to anybody, I hurried out, and jumped into a cab at the door, accompanied by the old professor from Liége, and the young Brussels lawyer.

It was a gorgeous day, about four o'clock in the afternoon, with brilliant sunlight flooding the city; and a feeling of intense elation came over me as our cab went rattling along over the old flagged streets.

Overhead, in the bright blue sky, aeroplanes were scouting. The wind blew sweet from the Scheldt, and the flat green lands beyond. All the banners stirred and waved. French, English, Belgian and Russian. And I felt contented, and glad I had started.

"First we call for Madame Julie!" said the young lawyer.

We drove along the quay, and stopped at a big white house.

To my surprise, I found myself now suddenly precipitated into the midst of a huge Belgian party, – mamma, papa, aunts, uncles, nephews, nieces, friends, officers, little girls, little boys, servants gathered in a great high-ceiled and be-windowed drawing-room crowded to the full. I was introduced to everybody, and a lot of handshaking went on.

I thought to myself, "This is a new way to get to Brussels!"

Servants were going round with trays laden with glasses of foaming champagne, and little sweet biscuits.

"We shall drink to the health of Julie!" said someone.

And we drank to Julie.

The sun poured in through the windows, and the genial affectionate Belgian family all gathered closer round the beloved daughter, who was going bravely back to-day to Brussels to join her husband there at his post.

It was a touching scene.

But as I think of it now, it becomes poignant with the tragedy hidden beneath the glittering sunlight and foaming champagne. That fine old man, with the dignified grey head and teard, was a distinguished Belgian minister, who has since met with a sad death. He was Julie's father, a father any woman might have been proud of. He said to me, "Je suis content that a lady is going too in this little company. It is hard for my daughter to be travelling about alone. Yet she is brave; she does not lack courage; she came alone all the way from Brussels three days ago in order to bring her little girl to Antwerp and leave her in our care. And now she feels it is her duty to go back to her husband in Brussels, though we, of course, long to have her remain with us."

Then at last the parting came, and tall, brown-eyed, buxom Julie kissed and was kissed by everybody, and everybody shook hands with me, and wished me luck, and I felt as if I was one with them, although I had never seen them in my life before, and never saw them in my life again.

We ran down the steps. And now, instead of getting into the old ricketty fiacre, we entered a handsome motor car belonging to the Belgian Ministry, and drove quickly to the quay. The father came with us, his daughter clinging to his arm. At the quay we went on board the big river steamer, and Julie bade her father farewell. She flung herself into his arms, and he clasped her tight. He held her in silence for a long minute. Then they parted.

They never met again.

As we moved away from the quay, it seemed to me that our steamer was steering straight for the Hesperides.

All the west was one great blazing field of red and gold, and the sun was low on the broad water's edge, while behind us the fair city of Antwerp lit sparkling lights in all her windows, and the old Cathedral rose high into the sunlight, with the Belgian banner fluttering from a pinnacle; and that is how I shall always see Antwerp, fair, and stately, and sun-wreathed, as she was that golden September afternoon.

When I think of her, I refuse to see her any other way!

I refuse to see her as she was when I came back to her.

Or as when I left her again for the Last Time.

CHAPTER X

FROM GHENT TO GRAMMONT

I don't know why we were all in such high spirits, for we had nothing but discomfort to endure.

And yet, out of that very discomfort itself, some peculiar psychic force seemed to spring to life and thrive, until we became as merry as crickets.

A more inherently melancholy type than the old Liége professor could scarcely be imagined.

Poor old soul!

He had lost his wife a week before the war, and in the siege of Liége one of his sons had fallen, and he had lost his home, and everything he held dear. He was an enormous man, dressed in deep black, the most pronounced mourning you can possibly imagine, with a great black pot-hat coming well down on his huge face. His big frame quivered like a jelly, as he sat in the corner of the train, and was shaken by the rough movements and the frequent stoppages. Yet he became cheerful, just as cheerful as any of us.

Strange as it seems in the telling, this cheerfulness is a normal condition of the people nearest the front. There is only one thing that kills it, loss of freedom when loss of freedom means loss of companionship. Ruin, danger, cold, hunger, heat, dirt, discomfort, wounds, suffering, death, are all dashed with glory, and become acceptable as part of the greatest adventure in the world. But loss of freedom wrings the colour from the brain, and shuts out this world and the next when it entails loss of comradeship.

When I first realised this strange phenomenon I thought it would take a volume of psychology to explain it.

And then, all suddenly, with no effort of thought, I found the explanation revealing itself in one magic blessed word, – *Companionship*.

Out here in the danger-zones, the irksome isolation of ordinary lives has vanished.

We are no longer alone; there are no such things as strangers; we are all together wherever we are; in the trenches, on the roads, in the trams, in the cities, in the villages, we all talk to each other, we all know each other's histories, we pour out our hopes and fears, we receive the warm, sweet stimulus of human comradeship multiplied out of all proportion to anything that life has ever offered any single one of us before, till even pain and death take on more gentle semblance seen with the eyes of a million people all holding hands.

Young men who have not gone, go now! Find out for yourselves whether this wonderful thing that I tell you is not true, that the battlefield, apart from its terrific and glorious qualities, holds also that secret of gaiety of heart that mankind is ever searching for!

We were at St. Nicolla now, and it was nearly dark, and our train was at a standstill.

"I'll get out and see what's the matter," said the young lawyer, whom I shall refer to hereafter as Jean.

He came back in a minute looking serious.

"The train doesn't go any further!" he said. "There's no train for Ghent to-night."

We all got out, clutching our bags, and stood there on the platform in the reddened dusk that was fast passing into night.

A Pontonnier, who had been in the train with us, came up and said he was expecting an automobile to meet him here, and perhaps he could give some of us a lift as far as Ghent.

However, his automobile didn't turn up, and that little plan fell through.

Jean began to bite his moustache and walk up and down, smiling intermittently, a queer distracted-looking smile that showed his white teeth.

He always did that when he was thinking how to circumvent the authorities. He had a word here with an officer, and a word there with a gendarme. Then he came back to us:

"We shall all go and interview the stationmaster, and see what can be done!"

So we went to the stationmaster, and Jean produced his papers, and Julie produced hers, and the old professor from Liége produced his, and I produced my English passport.

Jean talked a great deal, and the station master shook his head a great deal, and there was an endless colloquy, such as Belgians dearly love; and just as I thought everything was lost, the stationmaster hastened off into the dark with a little lantern and told us to follow him right across the train lines, and we came to a bewildering mass of lights, and at last we reached a spot in the middle of many train lines which seemed extremely dangerous, when the stationmaster said, "Stand there! And when train 57 comes along get immediately into the guard's van! There is only one."

We waited a long time, and the night grew cold and dark before 57 came along.

When it puffed itself into a possible position we all performed miracles in the way of climbing up an enormous step, and then we found ourselves in a little wooden van, with one dim light burning, and one wooden seat, and in we got, seating ourselves in a row on the hard seat, and off we started through the night for Ghent.

Looking through a peep-hole, I suddenly stifled an exclamation.

Pointing straight at me were the muzzles of guns.

"Mais oui,"said Jean. "That is what this train is doing. It is taking guns to Ghent. There are big movements of troops going on."

We were shaken nearly to pieces.

And we went so slowly that we scarcely moved at all.

But we arrived at Ghent at last, arrived of course, as usual in war timej at a station one had never seen or heard of before, in a remote, far-off portion of the town, and then we had to find our way back to the town proper, a long, long walk. It was twelve o'clock when we got into the beautiful old dream-like town.

First we went to the Hotel Ganda.

"Full up!" said the fat, white-faced porter rudely. "No room even on the floor to sleep."

"Can you give us something to eat?" we pleaded.

"Impossible! The kitchens are shut up."

He was a brute of a porter, an extraordinary man who never slept, and was on duty all night and all day.

He was hand in glove with the Germans all the time, his face did not belie him; he looked the ugliest, stealthiest creature, shewing a covert rudeness towards all English-speaking people, that many of us remember now and understand.

In the pitch darkness we set out again, clattering about the flagged streets of Ghent, a determined little party now, with our high spirits quite unchecked by hunger and fatigue, to try to find some sleeping place for the night.

From hotel to hotel we wandered; everyone was full; evidently a vast body of troops had arrived at Ghent that day. But, finally, at one o'clock we went last of all to the hotel we should have gone to first.

That was the Hotel de la Poste. It being the chief hotel at Ghent, we had felt certain it would be impossible to get accommodation there. But other people had evidently thought so too, and the result was we all got a room.

From the outside, the hotel appeared to be in pitch darkness, but when we got within we found lights burning, and great companies of Belgian cavalry officers gathered in the lounge, and halls, finishing their supper.

"There are great movements of troops going on," said Jean. "This is the first time I have seen our army in Ghent."

To my delight I recognised my two friends from. Aerschot, the "Brussels nuts."

On hearing that I was going to Brussels one of them begged me to go and see his father and sister, if I got safely there. And I gladly promised to do so.

After that (about two o'clock in the morning it was then) we crawled down some steps into the, cellar, where the most welcome supper I have ever eaten soon pulled us all round again. Cold fowl, red wine, delicious bread and butter. Then we went up to our rooms, giving strict injunctions to be called at six o'clock, and for four hours we slept the sleep of the thoroughly tired out.

Next morning at half-past six, we were all down, and had our cafe-au-lait in the restaurant, and then started off cheerfully to the principal railway station.

So far so good!

All we had to do now was to get into a train and be carried straight to Brussels.

Why, then, did Jean look so agitated when we went to the ticket office and asked for our tickets?

He turned to us with a shrug.

"Ah! Ces allemands! One never knows what the cochons are going to do! The stationmaster here says that the trains may not run into Brussels to-day. He won't book us further than Grammont! He believes the lines are cut from there on!"

I was so absorbed in watching the enormous ever-increasing crowds on the Ghent station that the seriousness of that statement passed me by. I did not realise where Grammont was. And it did not occur to me to wonder by what means I was going to get from Grammont to Brussels. I only urged that we should go on.

The old Professor and Madame Julie argued as to whether it would not be better to abandon their plans and return to Antwerp.

That seemed to me a tedious idea, so I did my best to push on.

Jean agreed.

"At any rate," he said, "we will go as far as Grammont and see what happens there. Perhaps by the time we get there we shall find everything alright again."

So at seven o'clock we steamed away from Ghent, out into the fresh bright countryside.

Now we were in the region of danger. We were outside the *derniere ligne* of the Belgian Army. If one came this way one came at one's risk. But as I looked from the train windows everything seemed so peaceful that I could scarcely imagine there was danger. There were no ruins here, there was no sign of War at all, only little farms and villages bathed in the blue September sunlight, with the peasants working in the fields.

As I tried to push my window higher, someone who was leaning from the next window, spoke to me in English, and I met a pair of blue English-looking eyes.

"May I fix that window for you? I guess you're English, aren't you, ma'am?"

I gave him one quick hard look.

It was the War Lotfk that raked a face with a lightning glance.

By now, I had come to depend absolutely on the result of my glance.

"Yes!" I said, "and you are American."

He admitted that was so.

Almost immediately we fell into talk about the War.

"How long do you think it will last?" asked the American.

"I don't know, what do you think?"

"I give it six weeks. I'll be over then."

And he assured me that was the general opinion of those he knew – six weeks or less.

"But what are you doing in this train?" he added interestedly.

"Going to Brussels!"

"Brussels!"

He looked at me with amazed eyes.

"Pardon me! Did you say going to Brussels?"

"Yes."

"Pardon me! But how are you going to get to Brussels?"

"I am going there."

"But you are English?"

"Yes."

"Then you can't have a German passport to get into Brussels if you are English."

"No. I haven't got one."

"But, don't you realise, ma'am, that to get into Brussels you have got to go through the German lines?"

We began to discuss the question.

He was an American who had friends in Brussels, and was going there on business. His name was Richards. He was a kindly nice man. He could speak neither French nor Flemish, and had a Belgian with him to interpret.

"What do you think I ought to do?" I asked.

"Go back," he promptly said. "If the Germans stop you, they'll take you prisoner. And even if you do get in," he added, "you will never get out! It is even harder to get out of Brussels than it is to get in."

"I'm going to chance it!"

"Well, if that's so, the only thing I can suggest is that if you do manage to get into Brussels safely, you go to the American Consulate, and shew them your papers, and they may give you a paper that'll help you to get out."

"But would the Americans do that for a British subject?"

"Sure! We're a neutral country. As a little American boy said, 'I'm neutral! I don't care which country whips the Germans!' "

Then another idea occurred to Mr. Richards.

"But you mustn't go into Brussels with an English passport about you. You'll have to hide that somehow!"

"I shall give it to Monsieur Jean to hide," I said. "He's the conductor of the little Belgian party there!"

"Well, let me see your passport! Then, in case you have to part with it, and you arrive in Brussels without it, I can satisfy our Consul that I have seen it, and that you are an English subject, and that will make things easier for you at the American Consulate."

I showed him my passport, and he examined it carefully and promised to do what he could to help me in Brussels.

Then we arrived at Grammont.
And there the worst happened.
The train lines were cut, and we could go no further by rail.
To get to Brussels we must drive by the roads all the way.

CHAPTER XI

BRABANT

It was like a chapter out of quite another story to leave the train at Grammont, and find ourselves in the flagged old Brabant square in front of the station, that hot glittering end-o'-summer morning, while on the ear rose a deafening babel of voices from the hundreds of little Belgian carts and carriages of all shapes and sizes and descriptions, that stood there, with their drivers leaning forward over their skinny horses yelling for fares.

The American hurried to me, as I stood watching with deep interest this vivacious scene, which reminded me of some old piazza in Italy, and quite took away the sharp edge of the adventure – the sharp edge being the Germans, who now were not very far away, judging by the dull roar of cannon that was here distinctly audible.

The American said: "Ma'am, I have found this little trap that will take us to Brussels for fourteen francs – right into Brussels, and there is a seat for you in that trap if you'd care to come. I'd be very pleased and happy to have you come along with me!"

"It is awfully good of you!" I said.

I knew he was running great risks in taking me with him, and I deeply appreciated his kindness.

But Jean remonstrated, a little hurt at the suggestion.

"Madame, you are of our party! We must stick together. I've just found a trap here that will take us all. There are four other people already in it, and that will make eight altogether. The driver will take us to Brussels for twelve francs each, with an extra five francs, if we get there safely!"

So I waved good-bye to the little cart with the friendly American, who waved back, as he drove away into the sunlight, shouting, "Good luck! "

"*Good luck!* "

As I heard that deep-sounding English word come ringing across the flagged old Brabant village, it was as though I realised its meaning for the first time.

"Good luck!"

And my heart clutched at it, and clung to it, searching for strength, as the heart of women – and men too – will do in war time!

CHAPTER XII

DRIVING EXTRAORDINARY

The task of arranging that party in the waggonette was anything but easy.

The old Liége professor, in his sombre black, sat on the back seat, while in front sat an equally enormous old banker from Brussels, also in black, and those two huge men seemed to stick up out of the carriage like vast black pillars.

They moved their seats afterwards, but it did not make any difference. Wherever they sat, they stuck up like huge black pillars, calling attention to us in what seemed to me a distinctly undesirable way.

Two horses we had for our long drive to Brussels, and uncommonly bony horses they were.

Our carriage was a species of long-drawn-out victoria.

It had an extra seat behind, with its back to the horses, a horrid, tilting little seat, as I soon discovered, for it was there that I found myself sitting, with Jean beside me, as we started off through the golden Saturday morning.

Jean and I had each to curl an arm round the back of the seat; otherwise we should have been tipped out; for a tremendously steep white hill-road, lined with poplars, began to rise before us, and we were in constant danger of falling forward on our noses.

But the only thing I cared about by then, was to sit next to Jean.

He seemed to be my only safeguard, my only hope of getting through this risky adventure.

And in low voices we discussed what I should do, if we did indeed meet the enemy, a contingency which began to grow more and more probable every moment.

All sorts of schemes were discussed between us, sitting there at the back of that jolting carriage.

But it was quite evident to both, that, though we might make up a plausible story as to why I was going to Brussels, although I might call myself an American, or an Italian, or a Spaniard (seeing that I could speak those languages well enough to deceive the Germans, and seeing also that I had the letter to the Spanish minister in my bag from the Vice-Consul at Antwerp), still, neither I nor Jean could do the one thing necessary; we could not produce any papers of mine that would satisfy the Germans if I fell into their hands.

"But we're not going to meet them!" said Jean.

He lit a cigarette.

"You had better give me all your papers," he added airily.

"What will you do with them?"

He smoked and thought.

"If we meet the Germans, I'll throw them away somewhere."

"But how on earth shall I ever get them again? And suppose the Germans see you throwing them away."

I did not like the phrase, "throw them away."

It seemed like taking from me the most precious thing in the world, the one thing that I had firmly determined never to part with – my passport!

But I now discovered that Jean had a thoughtful mood upon him, and did not want to talk. He' wanted to think. He told me so.

He said, "It is necessary that I think out many little things now! Pardon!"

And he tapped his brow.

So I left him to it!

Along the white sun-bathed road, as we drove, we met a continual procession of carts, waggons, fiacres, and vehicles of all shapes, kinds, and descriptions, full of peasants or bourgeoisie, all travelling in the direction of Ghent. Every now and then a private motor car would flash past us, flying the red, white and blue flag of Holland, or the Stars and Stripes of America. They had an almost impudent insouciance with them, those lucky neutral motor cars, as they rushed along the sunny Brabant road to Brussels, joyously confident that there would be no trouble for them if they met the Germans!

How I envied them! How I longed to be able by some magic to prove myself American or Dutch!

Every ten minutes or so we used to shout to people on the road, coming from the opposite direction.

"Il y a des Allemands?" or

"Il y a de danger?"

The answer would come back:

"Pas des Allemands!" or

"Out, les Allemands sont là" pointing to the right. Or

"Les Allemands sont là," pointing to the left.

I would feel horribly uncomfortable then.

Although apparently I was not frightened in the least, there was one thing that undeceived me about myself.

I had lost the power to think as clearly as usual.

I found that my brain refused to consider what I should do if the worst came to the worst. Whenever I got to that point my thoughts jibbed. Vagueness seized upon me.

I only knew that I was in for it now: that I was seated there in that old rickety carriage; that I was well inside the German lines; and that it was too late to turn back.

In a way it was a relief to feel incapable of dealing with the situation, because it set my mind free to observe the exquisite beauty of the country we were travelling through, and the golden sweetness of that never-to-be-forgotten September day.

Up and up that long steep white hill our carriage climbed, with rows of wonderful high poplars waving in the breeze on either side of us, and gracious grey Belgian chateaux shewing their beautiful lines through vistas of flower-filled gardens, and green undulating woods, of such richness, and fertility, and calm happy opulence, that the sound of the cannon growing ever louder across the valleys almost lost its meaning in such a fair enchanted country. But the breeze blew round us, a soft and gentle breeze, laden with the scent of flowers and green things. Red pears of great size and mellowness hung on the orchard trees. The purple cabbage that the Brabant peasants cultivate made bright spots along the ground. In the villages, at the doors of the little white cottages I saw old wrinkled Belgian women sitting. Little fair-haired, blue-eyed children, with peculiarly small, sweet faces, stood looking up and down the long roads with an expression that often brought the tears to my eyes as I realised the fears that those poor little baby hearts must be filled with in those desperate days.

And yet the prevailing note of the people we met along that road was still gaiety, rather than sadness or terror.

"*Il y a des Allemands?*"

"*Il y a de danger?*"

We went on perpetually with our questions, and the answers would come back laughingly with shakings of the head.

"No! Not met any Germans!" or:

"They are fighting round Ninove. We've been making detours all the morning to try and get out of their way!"

And now the road was so steep, that Jean and I jumped down from our sloping seat at the back and walked up the hill to save the bony horses.

Every now and then, we would pause to look back at that wide dreamlike view, which grew more and more magnificent the higher we ascended, until at last fair Brabant lay stretched out behind us, bathed in a glittering sunlight that had in it, that day, some exquisitely poignant quality as though it were more golden than gold, just because, across that great plain to the left, the fierce detonations of heavy artillery told of the terrific struggles that were going on there for life and death.

Presently we met a couple of black-robed Belgian priests walking down the hill, and mopping their pale faces under their black felt hats.

"The Germans are all over the place to-day," they told us. "And yesterday they arrested a train-full of people between Enghien and Hall.
They suspected them of carrying letters into Brussels. So they cut the
train lines last night, and marched the people off to be searched. The
young men have been sent into Germany to-day. Or so rumour says.
That may or may not be true. But anyway it is quite true that the
train-load of passengers was arrested wholesale, and that every single
one of them was searched, and those who were found carrying letters
were taken prisoners. Perhaps to be shot."

"*C'est ca!*" said Jean coolly.

We bade the priests good-bye, and trudged on.

Jean presently under his breath, said:

"I've got a hundred letters in my pockets. I'm taking them from
Antwerp people into Brussels. I suppose I shall have to leave them
somewhere!"

He smiled, his queer high-up smile, showing all his white teeth,
and I felt sure that he was planning something, I felt certain he was
not going to be baulked.

At the top of the hill we got into our trap again, and off we started, travelling at a great rate.

We dashed along, and vehicles dashed past us in the opposite direction, and I had the feeling that I was going for a picnic, so bright was
the day, so beautiful the surroundings, so quick the movements along
the road.

"At Enghien," said Jean, turning round and addressing the other
people in the carriage (by now they had all made friends with each
other, and were chattering nineteen to the dozen), "at Enghien we
shall get lunch!"

"But there is nowhere that one finds lunch at Enghien," protested
the fat Brussels banker.

"I promise you as good a lunch as ever you have eaten, and good
wine to wash it down!" was Jean's reply.

At last we arrived at Enghien, and found ourselves in a little brown
straggling picturesque village on a hillside, full of peasants, who were

gathered in a dense crowd in the "grand place," which was here the village common.

They had come in out of the fields, these peasants, stained with mud and all the discolourations of the soil. Their innocent faces spoke of the calm sweet things of nature. But mixed with the innocence was a great wonder and bewilderment now.

All this time, ever since we left Ghent, we had never seen a Belgian *militaire*.

That of itself told its own story of how completely we were outside the last chance of Belgian protection – outside *la derniere ligne*.

CHAPTER XIII

THE LUNCH AT ENGHIEN

Dear little Enghien! I shall always remember you.

It was so utterly-out-of-the-ordinary to drive to the railway station, and have one's lunch cooked by the stationmaster.

A dear old man he was, that old grey-bearded Belgian.

A hero too!

His trains were stopped; his lines were cut; he was ever in the midst of the Germans, but he kept his bright spirits happy, and when Jean ushered us all in to his little house that formed part of the railway station, he received us as if we were old friends, shook us all by the hand, and told us, with great gusto, exactly what he would give us.

And he rolled the words out too, almost as though he was an Italian, as he promised us a *bonne omelette,* followed by a *bon bif-steak*, and fried potatoes, and cheese, and fruit and a *bon café*!

Then he hurried away into the kitchen, and we heard him cracking the eggs, while his old sister set the table in the little dining-room.

We travellers all sat on a seat out in front of the railway line, under the sweet blue sky, facing green fields, and refreshed ourselves with little glasses of red, tonic-like Byrrh.[6]

It was characteristic of those dear Belgian souls that they one and all raised their little glasses before they drank, and looking towards

---

[6] *Byrrh* is a wine-based apéritif very popular back in the days, especially in french-speaking regions.

me said, *"Vive l'Angleterre!"*

To which I responded with my tiny glass, *"Leve la Belgique!"*

And we all added, *"A bas le Kaiser!"*

And from across the fields the noise of the battle round Ninove came towards us, louder and louder every moment.

As we sat there we discussed the cannonading that now seemed very near.

So loud and so close to us were the angry growl-lings of the guns that I felt amazed at not being able to see any smoke.

It was evident that some big encounter was going on, but the fields were green and still, and nothing at all was to be seen.

By now I had lost all sense of reality.

I was merely a figure in an extraordinary dream, in which the great guns pounded on my right hand, and the old stationmaster's omelette fried loudly on my left.

Jean strolled off alone, while two of the ladies of the party went away to buy some butter.

In Brussels, they said, it was impossible to get good butter under exorbitant prices, so they paid a visit to a little farm a few steps away, and came back presently laden with butter enough to keep them going for several weeks, for which they had paid only one franc each.

And now the old stationmaster comes out and summons us all in to lunch.

He wishes us *"bon appétit"* and we seat ourselves round the table under the portraits of King Albert and *"la petite reine!"* in his little sitting-room.

A merrier lunch than that was never eaten. The vast omelette melt-ed away in a twinkling before the terrific onslaught made upon it, chiefly by the Liége professor and the Brussels banker, who by now had got up their appetites.

The Red Cross lady, who took it upon herself to help out the food, kept up a cheerful little commentary of running compliments which included us all, and the beef-steak, and the omelette, and the pota-toes, and the stationmaster, until we could hardly tell one from the other, so agreeable did we all seem!

The old stationmaster produced some good Burgundy, sun-kissed, purply red of a most respectable age.

When everything was on the table he brought his chair and joined in with us, asking questions about Antwerp, and Ghent, and Ostend, and giving us in return vivid sketches of what the Germans had been doing in his part of the world. The extraordinary part of all this was that though we were in a region inhabited by the Germans there was no sign of destruction. The absence of ruin and pillage seems to conceal the fact that this was invested country.

After our *bon café* we all shook hands with the stationmaster, wished him good luck, and hurried back to the village, where we climbed into our vehicle again.

This time I took a place in the inside of the carriage, leaving Jean and another man to hang on to that perilous back seat.

At two o'clock we were off.

The horses, freshened by food and water, galloped along now at a great pace, and the day developed into an afternoon as cloudless and glittering as the morning.

But almost immediately after leaving Enghien an ominous note began to be struck.

Whenever we shouted out our query:

"Il y a des Allemands?" the passers-by coming from the opposite direction shouted back,

"Oui, oui, beaucoup d'Allemands!"

And suddenly there they were!

CHAPTER XIV

WE MEET THE GREY-COATS

My first sight of the German Army was just one man.

He was a motor cyclist dressed in grey, with his weapons slung across his back, and he flashed past us like lightning.

Everyone in the carriage uttered a deep "Oh!"

It seemed to me an incredible thing that one German should be all alone like that among enemies. I said so to my companions.

"The others are coming!" they said with an air of certainty that turned me cold all over.

But it was at least two miles further on before we met the rest of his corps.

Then we discovered fifty German motor cyclists, in grey uniforms, and flat caps, flying smoothly along the side path in one long grey line.

Their accoutrements looked perfect and trim, their general appearance was strikingly smart, natty, and workmanlike in the extreme.

Just before they reached us Jean got down and walked on foot along the road at the edge of the side path where they were riding.

And as they passed quite near him Jean turned his glance towards me and gave me an enormous wink.

I don't know whether that was Jean's sense of humour.

I always forgot afterwards to ask him what it meant.

I only know that it had a peculiarly cheering effect on me to see that great black eye winking and then turning itself with a quiet, careless gaze on the faces of the fifty German cyclists.

They passed without doing more than casting a look at us, and were lost to sight in a moment flashing onwards with tremendous speed towards Enghien.

We were now on the brow of a hill, and as we reached it, and began to descend, we were confronted with a spectacle that fairly took away my breath.

The long white road before us was literally lined with Germans.

CHAPTER XV

FACE TO FACE WITH THE HUNS

Yes, there they were! And when I found myself face to face with those five hundred advancing Germans, about two kilometres out of Enghien, I quite believed I was about to lose my chance of getting to Brussels and of seeing the man I was so anxious to see. Little did I dream at that moment, out there on the sunny Brabant hillside, seated in the old voiture, with that long, never-ending line of Germans filling the tree-lined white dusty highway far and wide with their infantry and artillery, their cannon, and the prancing horses of their officers, and their gleaming blue and scarlet uniforms, and glittering appointments, that it was not I who was going to be taken prisoner by "les Allemands" that brilliant Saturday afternoon, but Max of Brussels himself.

Up and down the long steep white road to Brussels the Germans halted, shouting in stentorian voices that we were to do likewise.

Our driver quickly brought his two bony horses to a standstill, and in the open carriage with me our queer haphazard party sat as if turned to stone.

The Red Cross Belgian lady had already hidden her Red Cross in her stocking, so that the Germans, if we met them, should not seize her and oblige her to perform Red Cross duties in their hated service.

The guttural voice of an erect old blue-and-scarlet German colonel fell on my ears like a bad dream, as he brought his big prancing grey horse alongside our driver and demanded roughly what we were doing there, while in the same bad dream, as I sat there in my corner of the voiture, I watched the expressions written all over those hundreds of fierce, fair, arrogant faces, staring at us from every direction.

In a blaze of hatred, I told myself that if ever the brute could be seen rampant in human beings' faces there it was, rampant, uncontrolled, unashamed, only just escaping from being degraded by the accompanying expressions of burning arrogance, and indomitable determination that blazed out of those hundreds of blue Teutonic eyes. The set of their lips was firm and grim beyond all words. Often a peculiar ironic smirk, caused by the upturning of the corners of their otherwise straight lips, seemed to add to their demoniac suggestiveness. But their physique was magnificent, and there was not a man among them who did not look every inch a soldier, from his iron-heeled blucher boots upwards.

As I studied them, drinking in the unforgettable picture, it gave me a certain amount of satisfaction to know that I was setting my own small womanly daring up against that great mass of unbridled cruelty and conceit, and I sat very still, very still indeed, stiller than any mouse, allowing myself the supreme luxury of a contemptuous curl of my lips. Picture after picture of the ruined cities I had seen in Belgium flashed like lightning over my memory out there on the sunny Brabant hillside. Again I saw before me the horrors that I had seen with my own eyes at Aerschot, Termonde, and Louvain, and then, instead of feeling frightened I experienced nothing but a red-hot scorn that entirely lifted me above the terrible stress of the encounter; and whether I lived or died mattered not the least bit in the world, beside the satisfaction of sitting there, an English subject looking down at the German Army, with that contemptuous curl of my lips, and that blaze of hatred in my heart.

Meanwhile our driver's passport with his photograph was being examined.

"Who is this?" shouted the silly old German Colonel, pointing to the photograph.

"C'est moi," replied the driver, and his expression seemed to say, "Who on earth did you think it was?"

The fat Colonel, who obviously did not understand a word of French, kept roaring away for one "Schultz," who seemed to be some distance off.

The roaring and shouting went on for several minutes.

It was a curious manifestation of German lack of dignity and I tried in vain to imagine an English Colonel roaring at his men like that.

Then "Schultz" came galloping up. He acted as interpreter, and an amusing dialogue went on between the roaring Colonel and the young dashing "Baverois," who was obviously a less brutal type than his interrogator.

The old banker from Brussels was next questioned, and his passport to come in and out of Brussels being correctly made out in German and French, the Germans seized upon Jean and demanded what he was doing there, why he was going to Brussels, and why he had been to Grammont. Jean's answer was that he lived in Brussels and had been to Grammont to see his relations, and "Schultz's" explanations rendered this so convincing that the lawyer's passport was handed back to him.

"You are sure none of you have no correspondence, no newspapers?" roared the Colonel. "What is in that bag?"

Leaning into the carriage a soldier prodded at *my* bag.

I dared not attempt to speak. My English origin might betray me in my French. I sat silent. I made no reply. I tried to look entirely uninterested. But I was really almost unconscious with dread.

But the Red Cross lady replied with quiet dignity that there was nothing in her bag but requisites for the journey.

Next moment, as in a dream, I heard that roaring voice shout: "Gut! Get on!"

Our driver whipped lightly, the carriage moved forward, and we proceeded on our way, filled with queer thoughts that sprang from nerves overstrained and hearts over-quickly beating.

Only Jean remained imperturbable.

"Quel Chance! They were nearly all Baverois! Did you see the dragon embroidered on their pouches? The Baverois are always plus gentilles than any of the others."

This was something I had heard over and over again. According to
the Belgians, these Baverois had all through the War, manifested a
better spirit towards the Belgians than any other German Regiment,
the accredited reason being, that the Belgian Queen is of Bavarian
nationality. When the Uhlans slashed up the Queen's portrait in the
Royal Palace at Brussels the "Baverois" lost their tempers, and a fierce
brawl ensued, in which seven men were killed. All the Belgians in our
old ramshackle carriage were loud in their expressions of thankfulness
that we had encountered Baverois instead of Uhlans.

So at last that dread mysterious darksome quantity known as "les
Allemands," ever moving hither and thither across Belgium, always
talked of on the other side of the Belgian lines, but never seen, had
materialised right under my very eyes!

The beautiful rich Brabant orchard country stretched away on
either side of the road, and behind us, along the road, ran like a wash
of indigo, the brilliant Prussian blue of the moving German cavalcade making now towards Enghien and Grammont.

And now the old professor from Liege drew all attention towards
himself.

He was shaking and quivering like a jelly.

"J'ai peur!" he said simply.

"Mais non, Monsieur!" cried Jean. "It's all over now."

"*Courage! courage! Pas de danger*" cried everyone, encouragingly.

"It was only a ruse of the enemy, letting us go," whispered the
Professor. "They will follow and shoot us from behind!"

Plaintively, as a child, he asked the fat Brussels banker to allow him
to change places, and sit in front, instead of behind.

In a sudden rebound of spirits, the Red Cross lady and I laughingly sat on the back seat, and opened our parasols behind us, while the
old Brussels banker, when the two fat men had exchanged seats not
without difficulty, whispered to us:

"And all the while there are a hundred letters sewn up inside the
cushion of the seat our friend from Liége is sitting on *now!*"

CHAPTER XVI

A PRAYER FOR HIS SOUL

On we drove, on and on.

All the road to Brussels was patrolled now. At the gates of villa gardens, on the side paths, grey German sentries were posted, bayonets fixed. We drove through Germans all the way. They looked at us quietly. Once only were we stopped again, and this time it was only the driver's passport that was looked at.

At last we arrived at Hall, an old-world Brabant town containing a "miracle." As far as I can remember, it was a bomb from some bygone War that came through the church wall and was caught in the skirts of the Madonna!

"Hall," said Jean, "is now the head-quarters of the German Army in Belgium! The Etat-Majeur has been moved here from Brussels. He is in residence at the Hotel de Ville. Voila! See the Germans. They always pose themselves like that on the steps where there are any steps to pose on. Ah, mais c'est triste n'est-ce-pas? Mon pauvre Belgique!"

We clattered up the main street and stopped at a little cafe, facing the Hotel de Ville.

Stiffly we alighted from our waggonette, and entering the cafe quenched our thirst in lemonade, watching the Germans through the window as we rested.

Nervous as I was myself, I admired the Belgians' sangfroid. They manifested not the slightest signs of nervousness. Scorn was their leading characteristic. Then a sad little story reached my ears. An old peasant was telling Jean that an English aviator had been shot down at Hall the day before, and was buried somewhere near.

How I longed to look for my brave countryman's grave! But that was impossible. Instead, I breathed a prayer for his soul, and thought of him and his great courage with tenderness and respect.

It was all I could do.

CHAPTER XVII

BRUSSELS

Finally, after a wild and breathless drive of thirty-five miles through rich orchard-country all the way, and always between German patrols, we entered Brussels. Crowds of German officers and men were dashing about in motor-cars in all directions, while the populace moved by them as though they were ghosts, taking not the slightest notice of their presence. The sunlight had faded now, and the lights were being lit in Brussels, and I gazed about me, filled with an inordinate curiosity. At first I thought the people seemed to be moving about just as usual, but soon I discovered an immense difference between these Brussels crowds, and those of normal times and conditions. It was as though all the red roses and carnations had been picked out of the garden. The smart world had completely disappeared. Those daintily-dressed, exquisite women, and elegant young and old men, that made such persuasive notes among the streets and shops of Brussels in ordinary times, had vanished completely under the German occupation. In their place was now a rambling, roaming crowd of the lower middle-classes, dashed with a big sprinkling of wide-eyed wrinkled peasants from the Brabant country outside, who had come into the big city for the protection of the lights and the houses and the companionship, even though the dreaded "Allemands" were there. Listlessly people strolled about. They looked in the shop windows, but nobody bought. No business seemed to be done at all, except in the provision shops, where I saw groups of German officers and soldiers buying sausages, cheese and eggs.

Crowds gathered before the German notices, pasted on the walls so continuously that Brussels was half covered beneath these great black and white printed declarations, which, as they were always printed in three languages – German, French and Flemish – took up an enormous amount of wall space. Here and there Dutch journalists stood hastily copying these "*affiches*" into their note-books. Now and then, from the crowd reading, a low voice would mutter languidly "Les sales cochons!" But more often the Brussels sense of humour would see something funny in those absurd proclamations, and people were often to be seen grinning ironically at the German official war news specially concocted for the people of Brussels. It was all the Direct Opposite of the news in Belgian and English papers. *We*, the Allies, had just announced that Austria had broken down, and was on the verge of a revolution. *They*, the Germans, announced precisely the same thing – only of Servia! And the Brussels people coolly read the news and passed on, believing none of it.

And all the time, while the Belgians moved dawdlingly up and down, and round about their favourite streets and arcades, the Germans kept up one swift everlasting rush, flying past in motors, or striding quickly by, with their firm, long tread. They always seemed to be going somewhere in a hurry, or doing something extraordinarily definite. After I had been five minutes in Brussels, I became aware of this curious sense of immense and unceasing German activity, flowing like some loud, swift, resistless current through the dull, depleted stream of Brussels life. All day long it went without ceasing, and all night too. In and out of the city, in and out of the city, in and out of the city. Past the deserted lace shops, with their exquisite delicate contents; past the many closed hotels; past the great white beauties of Brussels architecture; past the proud but yellowing avenues of trees along the heights; past those sculptured monuments of Belgians who fell in bygone battles, and now, in the light of 1914, leapt afresh into life again, galvanised back into reality by the shriek of a thousand *obus*, and the blood poured warm on the blackened fields of Belgium.

We drove to an old hotel in a quiet street, and our driver jumped down and rang the courtyard bell.

Then the door opened, and an old Belgian porter stood and looked at us with sad eyes, saying in a low voice, "Come in quickly!"

We all got down and went through the gateway.

We found ourselves in a big old yellow stone courtyard, chilly and deserted.

The driver ran out and returned, carrying in his arms the long flat seat-cushion from the carriage.

Then the old porter locked the gate and we all gathered round the brave little Flemish driver who was down on his knees now, over the cushion, doing something with a knife.

Next minute he held up a bundle of letters, and then another and then another, –

"And here is your English passport, Madame," Jean said to me.

Unknown to most of us, the driver and Jean, while we waited at Enghien, had made a slit in the cushion, had taken out some stuffing, and put in instead a great mass of letters and papers for Brussels, then they had wired up the slit, turned the cushion upside down, and let us sit on it.

It was rather like sitting on a mine.

Only, like the heroine of the song: "We didn't care, we didn't KNOW!"

CHAPTER XVIII

BURGOMASTER MAX

The hotel is closed to the public.

"We shut it up so that we should not have Germans coming in," says the little Bruxellois widow who owns it. "But if Madame likes to stay here for the night we can arrange, – only – there is no cooking!"

The old professor from Liege asks in his pitiful childlike way if he can get a room there too. He would be glad, so glad, to be in a hotel that was not open to the public, or the Germans.

Leaving my companions with many expressions of friendliness, I now rush off to the Hotel de Ville, accompanied by the faithful Jean.

Just as we reach our destination, we run into the man I have come all this way to see.

I see a short, dark man, with an alert military bearing. It seems to me that this idol of Brussels is by no means good-looking. Certainly, there is nothing of the hero in his piquant, even somewhat droll appearance. But his eyes! They are truly extraordinary! They bulge right out of their sockets. They have the sharpness and alertness of a terrier's. They are brilliant, humorous stern, merry, tender, audacious, glistening, bright all at once. His beard is clipped. His moustaches are large and upstanding. His immaculate dress and careful grooming give him a dandified air, as befitting the most popular bachelor in Europe, who is also an orphan to boot. His forehead is high and broad. His general appearance is immediately arresting, one scarcely knows why. Quite unlike the conventional Burgomaster type is he.

M. Max briefly explains that he is on his way to an important meeting. But he will see me at eleven o'clock next morning if I will come to the Hotel de Ville. Then he hurries off, his queer dark face lighting up with a singularly brilliant smile as he bids us "Au revoir!" An historic moment that. For M. Max has never been seen in Brussels since!

Of itself, M. Max's face is neither particularly loveable, nor particularly attractive.

Therefore, this man's great hold over hearts is all the more remarkable.

It must, of course, be attributed in part to the deep, warm audacious personality that dwells behind his looks.

But, in truth, M. Max's enormous popularity owes itself not only to his electric personality, his daring, and sangfroid, but also to his *commonsense*, which steered poor bewildered Brussels through those terribly difficult first weeks of the German occupation.

Nothing in history is more touching, more glorious, than the sudden starting up in time of danger of some quiet unknown man who stamps his personality on the world, becomes the prop and comfort of his nation, is believed in as Christians believe in God, and makes manifest again the truth that War so furiously and jealously attempts to crush and darken – the power of mind over matter, the mastery of good over evil.

From this War three such men stand out immortally – King Albert, Max of Brussels, Mercier of Malines.[7]

And Belgium has produced all three!

Thrice fortunate Belgium!

Each stone that crumbles from her ruined homes seems, to the watching world, to fly into the Heavens, and glow there like a star!

On foot, swinging my big yellow furs closer round me in the true Belgian manner, I walked along at Jean's side, trying to convince myself that this was all real, this Brussels full of grey-clad and blue-

---

[7] Desiré-Félicien-François-Joseph Mercier (1851-1926), Archbishop of Mechelen from 1906 until his death, writer and theologian.

clad Prussians, Saxons, and Baverois, with here and there the white uniform of the Imperial Guard. Suddenly I started. Horribly conscious as I was that I was an English authoress and with no excuse to offer for my presence there I felt distinctly nervous when I saw a queer young man in a bulky brown coat move slowly along a my side with a curious sidling movement whispering something under his breath.

I was not sure whether to hurry on, or to stand still.

Jean chose the latter course.

Whereupon the stranger flicked a look up and down the street, then put his hand in his inner breast pocket.

"*Le Temps*," he whispered hoarsely, flashing looks up and down the street.

"How much?" asked Jean.

"Five francs," he answered. "Put it away toute suite, vous savez c'est dangereux."

Then quickly he added, walking along beside us still, and speaking still in that hoarse, melodramatic voice (which pleased him a little, I couldn't help thinking), "Les Allemands will give me a year in prison if they catch me, so I have to make it pay, n'est-ce-pas? But the Brussels people *must* have their newspapers. They've got to know the truth about the war, n'est-ce-pas? and the English papers tell the truth!"

"How do you get the newspapers," I whispered, like a conspirator myself.

"I sneak in and out of Brussels in a peasant's cart, all the way to Sottegem," he whispered back. "Every week they catch one of us. But still we go on – n'est-ce-pas? We don't know what fear is in Brussels. That's because we've got M. Max at the head of us! Ah, there's a man for you, M. Max!"

A look of pride and tenderness flashed across his dark, crafty face, then he was gone, and I found myself longing for the morning, when I should talk with M. Max myself.

But Sunday I was awakened by the loud booming of cannon, proceeding from the direction of Malines.

"What is happening?" I asked the maid who brought my coffee "Isn't that firing very near?"

"Oui, Madam! On dit that in a few days now the Belgian Army will re-enter Brussels, and the Germans will be driven out. That will be splendid, Madam, will it not?"

"Splendid," I answered mechanically.

This optimism was now becoming a familiar phrase to me.

I found it everywhere. But alas! I found it alongside what was continually being revealed as pathetic ignorance of the true state of affairs.

And the nearer one was to actual events the greater appeared one's ignorance.

This very day, when we were saying, "In a few days now the Germans will be driven out of Brussels," they were commencing their colossal attack upon Antwerp, and we knew nothing about it.

The faithful Jean called for me at half-past ten, and hurrying through the rain-wet streets to meet M. Max at the Hotel de Ville, we became suddenly aware that something extraordinary was happening. A sense of agitation was in the air. People were hurrying about, talking quickly and angrily. And then our eyes were confronted by the following startling notice, pasted on the walls, printed in German, French and Flemish, and flaming over Brussels in all directions: –

AVIS.

Le Bourgmestre Max ayant fait default aux engagements encourus envers le Gouvernment Allemand je me suis vu force de le suspendre de ses fonctions. Monsieur Max se trouve en detention honourable dans une forteresse.

Le Gouverneur Allemande,
VON DER GOLTZ.
Bruxelles, *26th Septembre*, 1914.

Cries of grief and rage kept bursting from those broken-hearted Belgians.

Not a man or woman in the city was there who did not worship the very ground Max walked on. The blow was sharp and terrible; it was utterly unexpected too. Crowds kept on gathering. Presently, with that never-ceasing accompaniment of distant cannon, the anger of the populace found vent in groans and hisses as a body of Uhlans made its appearance, conducting two Belgian prisoners towards the Town Hall. And then, all in a moment, Brussels was in an uproar. Prudence and fear were flung to the wind. Like mad creatures the seething crowds of men, women, and children went tearing along towards the Hotel de Ville, groaning and hooting at every German they saw, and shouting aloud the name of "Max," while to add to the indescribable tumult, hundreds of little boys ran shrieking at the tops of their voices, "*Voici le photographie ed Monsieur Max, dix centimes!*"

The Civic Guard, composed now mostly of elderly enrolled Brussels civilians, dashed in and out among the infuriated mob, waving their sticks, and imploring the population to restrain itself, or the consequences might be fatal for one and all.

Meanwhile the Aldermen were busy preparing a new *affiche* which was soon being posted up in all directions.

AVIS IMPORTANT.

Pendant l'absence de M. Max le marche des affaires Communales et le Maintenance de l'ordre seront assurés par le College Echevinal. Dans l'interet de la cité nous faisons un supreme appel au calme et sangfroid de nos concitoyens. Nous comptons sur le concours de tous pour assurer le maintien de la tranquilité publique.

LE COLLEGE ECHEVINAL.
Bruxelles.

Accompanied by Jean, I hurried on to the Hotel de Ville.

"Voyez vous!" says Jean under his breath. "Voici les Allemands dans l'Hotel de Ville! Quel chose n'est-ce-pas!"

And I hear a sharp note in the poor fellow's voice that told of bitter emotion.

It was an ordeal to walk through that beautiful classic courtyard, patrolled by grey-clad German sentinels armed to the teeth. The only thing to do was to pass them without either looking or not looking. But once inside I felt safer. The Germans kept to their side of the Town Hall, leaving the Belgian Municipality alone. We went up the wide stairs, hung with magnificent pictures and found a sad group of Belgians gathered in a long corridor, the windows of which looked down into the courtyard below where the Germans were unloading waggons, or striding up and down with bayonets fixed.

Looking down from that window, while we waited to be received by M. le Meunier, the Acting-Burgomaster who had promptly taken M. Max's place, I interested myself in studying the famous German leg. A greater part of it was boot. These boots looked as though immense attention had been given to them. In fact there was nothing they didn't have, iron heels, waterproof uppers, patent soles an immense thickness, with metal intermingled, an infinite capacity for not wearing out. I watched these giant boots standing in the gateway of the exquisite Hotel de Ville, fair monument of Belgium's genius for the Gothic! I could see nothing of the upper part of the Germans, only their legs, and it was forced upon my observation that those legs were of great strength and massive, yet with a curious flinging freedom of gait, that was the direct result of goose-stepping.

Then I saw two officers goose-stepping into the courtway. I saw their feet first! then their knees. The effect was curious. They appeared to kick out contemptuously at the world, then pranced in after the kick. The conceit of the performance defies all words.

Then Jean's card was taken into the acting Burgomaster, and next moment a Belgian Échevin said to us, "Entrez, s'il vous plait," and we passed into the room habitually occupied by M. Max.

We found ourselves in a palatial chamber, the walls covered thickly with splendid tapestries and portraits. From the high gilded ceiling

hung enormous chandeliers, glittering and pageantesque. Under one
of these giant chandeliers stood an imposing desk covered with
papers. An elderly gentleman with a grey wide beard was seated there.
We advanced over the thick soft carpets.

M. le Meunier received us with great courtesy.

"Nous avons perdu notre tête!" he murmured sadly. – "Without M.
Max we are lost!"

The air was full of agitation.

Here was a scene the like of which might well have been presented
by the stage, so spectacular was it, so dramatic – the lofty chamber
with its superb appointments and hangings, and these elderly, grey-
bearded men of state who had just been dealt the bitterest blow that
had yet fallen on their poor tortured shoulders.

But this was no stage scene. This was real. If ever anything on earth
was alive and real it was this scene in the Burgomaster's room in
Brussels, on the first day of Max's imprisonment. Throbbing and pal-
pitating through it was human agony, human grief, human despair,
as these grey-bearded Belgians stared with dull heavy eyes at the
empty space where their heroic chief no longer was. Tragic beyond
the words of any historian was that scene, which at last however, by
sheer intensity of concentrated and concealed emotion, seemed to
summon again intotthat chamber the imprisoned body, the blazing,
dauntless personality of the absent one, until his prison bonds were
broken, and he was here, seated at this desk, cool, fearless, imperturbable, directing the helm of his storm-tossed bark with his splendid sanity, and saying to all:

"Fear nothing, mes enfants! There is no such thing as fear!"

CHAPTER XIX

HIS ARREST

The story of Max's arrest was characteristic.

He was busy at the Hotel de Ville with his colleagues when a peremptory message arrived from Von der Goltz, bidding him come at once to an interview.

"I cannot come at once!" said Max, "I am occupied in an important conference with my colleagues. I'll come at half-past four o'clock."

Presently the messenger returned.

"Monsieur Max, will you come at once!" he said in a worried manner. "Von der Goltz is angry!"

"I am busy with my work!" replied Max imperturbably. "As I said before, I shall be with Von der Goltz at four-thirty."

At four-thirty he went off, accompanied by his colleagues, and a dramatic conference took place between the Germans and Belgians.

Max now fearlessly informed the Germans that he considered it would be unfair for Brussels to pay any more at present of the indemnity put upon it by Germany.

One reason he gave was very simple.

The Germans had posted up notices in the city, declaring that in future they would not pay for anything required for the service of the German Army, but would take whatever they wanted, free.

"You must wait for your indemnity," said Max. "You can't get blood from a stone."

"Then we arrest you all as hostages for the money," was the

German's answer.

At first Max and all his Echevins were arrested.

Two hours later the aldermen were released.

But not Max.

He was sent to his *honorable detention* in a German fortress.

The months have passed.

He is still there!

CHAPTER XX

GENERAL THYS

By degrees Brussels calmed down. But the Germans wore startled expressions all that grey wet Sunday, as though realising that within that pent-up city was a terribly dangerous force, a force that had been restrained and kept in order all this time by the very man they had been foolish enough to imprison because Brussels found herself unable to pay up her cruelly-imposed millions.

Later, on that Sunday afternoon, I fulfilled my promise and went to call on General Thys, the father of one of my Aerschot acquaintances.

I found the old General in that beautiful house of his in the Chausee de Charleroi, sitting by the fireside in his library reading the Old Testament.

"The only book I can read now!" the General said, in a voice that shook a little, as if with some burning secret agitation.

I remember so well that interview. It was a grey Sunday afternoon, with a touch of autumn in the air, and no sunlight. Through the great glass windows at the end of the library I could see that Brussels garden, with some trees green, and some turning palely gold, already on their way towards decay.

Seated on one side of the fire was the beautiful young unmarried daughter of the house, sharing her father's terrible loneliness, while on the other side sat the handsome melancholy old Belgian hero, whose trembling voice began presently to tell the story of his beloved nation, its suffering, its heroism, its love of home, its bygone struggles for liberty.

And outside in the streets Germans strode up and down, Germans stood on the steps of the Palais de Justice, Germans everywhere.

Mademoiselle Thys, a tall, fair, very beautiful young girl, chats away brightly, trying to cheer her father. Presently she talks of M. Max. Brussels can talk of nothing else to-day. She shows him to me in a different aspect. Now I see him in society, witty, delightful, charming, débonnaire.

"I did so love to be taken into dinner by M. Max!" exclaims the bright young belle. "He was so interesting, so amusing. And so nice to flirt with. He did not dance, but he went to all the balls, and walked about chatting and amusing himself, and everyone else. Before one big fancy dress ball – it was the last in Brussels before the war – M. Max announced that he could not be present. Everyone was sorry. His presence always made things brighter, livelier. Suddenly, in the midst of the ball a policeman was seen coming up the stairs, his stick in his hand. Gravely, without speaking to anyone he moved down the corridors. 'The Police' whispered everyone. 'can it mean?' And then one of the hosts went up to the policeman, determined to take the bull by the horns, as you say in Angleterre, and find out what is wrong. And voila! It is no policeman at all. It is M. Max!"

Undoubtedly, the hatred and terror of Germany at this time was all for Russia.

In Russia, Germany saw her deadliest foe. Every Belgian man or woman that I talked with in Brussels asserted the same thing. "The Germans are terrified of Russia," said the old General. "They see in Russia the greatest enemy to their plans in Asia Minor. They fear Russian civilisation – or so they say! Civilisation indeed! What they fear is Russian numbers!"

It was highly interesting to observe as I was forced to do a little later, how completely that hatred for Russia was passed on to England.

The passing on occurred *after English troops were sent to the assistance of Antwerp!*

From then on, the blaze of hatred in Germany's heart was all for England, deepening and intensifying with extraordinary ferocity ever since October 4th, 1914.

And why? The reason is obvious now.

Our effort to save Antwerp, unsuccessful as it was, yet by delaying 200,000 Germans, enabled those highly important arrangements to be carried out on the Allies' western front that frustrated Germany's hopes in France, and stopped her dash for Calais!

CHAPTER XXI

HOW MAX HAS INFLUENCED BRUSSELS

In their attitude to the Germans, the *Bruxellois* undoubtedly take their tone from M. Max.

For his sake they suppressed themselves as quickly as possible that famous Sunday and soon went on their usual way. Their attitude towards the Germans revealed itself as a truly remarkable one. It was perfect in every sense. They were never rude, never sullen, never afraid, and until this particular Sunday and afterwards again, they always behaved as though the Germans did not exist at all. They walked past them as though they were air.

No one ever speaks to the Huns in Brussels. They sit there alone in the restaurants, or in groups, eating, eating, eating. Hour after hour they sit there. You pass at seven and they are eating and drinking. You pass at nine, they are still eating and drinking. Their red faces grow redder and redder. Their gold wedding rings grow tighter and tighter on their fingers.

The Belgians wait on them with an admirable air of not noticing their presence, never looking at them, never speaking to them, the waiters bringing them their food with an admirable detached air as though they are placing viands before a set of invisible spectres.

Always alone are the Germans in Brussels, and sometimes they look extremely bored. I can't help noticing that.

They do their best to win a little friendliness from the Belgians. But in vain. At the restaurants they always pay for their food. They also make a point of sometimes ostentatiously dropping money into the boxes for collecting funds for the Belgians. But the *Bruxellois* never for one moment let down the barriers between themselves and "les Allemands," although they do occasionally allow themselves the joy of "getting a rise" out of the Landsturm when possible, – an amusement which the Germans apparently find it impolite to resent!

I sat in a tram in Brussels when two Germans in mufti entered and quite politely excused themselves from paying their fares, explaining that they were "military" and travel free.

"But how do I know that you are really German soldiers!" says the plucky little tram guard, while all the passengers crane forward to listen. "You're not in uniform. I don't know who you are. You must pay your fares, Messieurs, or you must get out."

With red annoyed faces the Germans pull out their soldiers' medals, gaudy ornate affairs on blue ribbons round their necks.

"I don't recognise these," says the tram guard, examining them solemnly. "They're not what our soldiers carry. I can't let you go free on these."

"But we have no money!" splutter the Germans.

"Then I must ask you to get out," says the guard gravely.

And the two Germans, looking very foolish, actually get out of the tram, whereupon the passengers all burst into uncontrollable laughter, which gives them a vast amount of satisfaction, while the two Germans, very red in the face, march away down the street.

As for the street urchins, they flourish under the German occupation, adopting exactly the same attitude towards their conquerors as that manifested by their elders and M. Max.

Dressed up in paper uniforms, with a carrot for the point of their imitation German helmet they march right under the noses of the Germans, headed by an old dog.

Round the old dog's neck is an inscription:

"The war is taking 'place for the aggrandisement of Belgium!"

The truth is – the beautiful truth – that the spirit of M. Max hangs over Brussels, steals through it, pervades it. It is his ego that possesses the town. It is Max who is really in occupation there. It is Max who is the true conqueror. It is Max who holds Brussels, and will hold it through all time to come. For all that the Germans are going about the streets, and for all that Max is detained in his "honorable" fortress, the man's spirit is so indomitable, so ardent, that he makes himself felt through his prison walls, and the population of Brussels is able to say, with magnificent sangfroid, and a confidence that is absolutely real: –

"They may keep M. Max in a fortress! But even les alboches will never dare to hurt a hair of his head!"

CHAPTER XXII

UNDER GERMAN OCCUPATION

In my empty hotel the profoundest melancholy reigns.

The inherent sadness of the occupied city seems to have full, sway here. The palm court, with its high glassed roof, is swept with ghostly echoes, especially when the day wanes towards dusk, the great deserted dining-salon, with its polished tables and its rows of chairs is like a mausoleum for dead revellers, the writing-rooms with their desks always so pitifully tidy, the smoking-rooms, the drawing-rooms, the floor upon floor of empty, guestless bedrooms, with the beds rolled back and the blinds down; they ache with their ghastly silences and seem to languish away towards decay.

The only servant is Antoine, the bent little old faithful white-haired porter, who has passed his life-time in the service of the house.

Madame la Patronne, in heavy mourning, with her two small boys clinging to either arm, sometimes moves across the palm court to her own little sitting-room.

And sometimes some Belgian woman friend, always in black, drops in, and she and la Patronne and the old porter all talk together, dully, guardedly, relating to each other the gossip of Brussels, and wondering always how things are going with "les petits Belges" outside in the world beyond.

In front, the great doors are locked and barred.

One tiny door, cut in the wooden gate at the side, is one's sole means of exit and entrance.

But it is almost too small for the Liége professor, and he tells me plaintively that he will be glad to move on to Liege.

"I get broken to pieces squeezing in and out of that little door," he says. "And I am always afraid I will stick in the middle, and the Germans in the restaurant will see me, and ask who I am, and what I am doing here!"

"I can get through the door easily enough," I answer. "But I suffer agonies as I stand there on the street waiting for old Antoine to come and unlock it."

"And then there is no food here, no lunch, no dinner, and I do not like to go in the restaurants alone; I am afraid the Germans will notice me. I am so big, you see, everybody notices me. Do you think I will ever get to Liége?"

"Of course you will."

"But do you think I will ever get back from Liége to Antwerp?"

"Of course you will."

"J'ai peur!"

"Moi aussi!"

And indeed, sitting there in the dusk, in the eerie silences of the deserted hotel, with the German guns booming away in the distance towards Malines, there creeps over me a shuddering sensation that is very like fear at the ever-deepening realization of what Belgium has suffered, and may have to suffer yet; and I find it almost intolerable – the thought of this poor brave old trembling Belgian, weighted with years and flesh, struggling so manfully to get back to Liége, and gauge for himself the extent of the damage done to his house and properties, to see his servants and help them make arrangements for the future. Like all the rest of the Belgian fugitives, he knows nothing *definite* about the destruction of his town. It may be that his home has been razed to the ground. It may be that it has been spared. He is sure of nothing, and that is why he has set out on this long and dangerous journey, which is not by any means over yet.

Then the old porter approaches, gentle, sorrowful.

"Monsieur, good news! there is a train for Liége to-morrow morning at five o'clock!"

"Merci bien,"says the old professor. "Mais, j'ai peur!"

I rise at four next morning and come down to see him off. We two, who have never seen each other before, seem now like the only relics of some bygone far-off event. To see his fat, old, enormous face gives me a positive thrill of joy. I feel as if I have known him all my life, and when he has gone I feel curiously alone. The melancholy old fat man's presence had lent a semblance of life to the hotel, which now seems given over to ghosts and echoes. Unable to bear it, I moved into the Métropole.

It was very strange to be there, very strange indeed! This was the Métropole and yet not the Métropole! Sometimes I could not believe it was the Métropole at all – the gay, bright, lively, friendly, companionable Métropole – so sad was this big red-carpeted hotel, so full of gloomy echoing silences, and with never a soul to arrive or leave, to ask for a room or a time-table.

There were Italians in charge of the hotel, for which I was profoundly thankful.

How nice they were to me, those kindly sons of the South.

They allowed me to look in their visitors' book, and as I expected, I found that the dry hotel register had suddenly become transformed into a vital human document, of surpassing interest, of intense historic value.

As I glanced through the crowded pages I came at last upon an ominous date in August upon which there were no names entered.

It was the day on which Brussels surrendered to the Germans.

On that day the register was blank, entirely blank.

And next day also, and the next, and the next, and the next, were those white empty sheets, with never a name inscribed upon them.

For weeks this blankness continued. It was stifling in its significance. It clutched at one's heart-strings. It shouted aloud of the agony of those days when all who could do so left Brussels, and only those who were obliged to remained. It told its desolate tale of the visitors that had fled, or ceased to come.

Only, here and there after a long interval, appeared a German name or two.

Frau Schmidt arrived; Herr Lemberg; Fraulein Gottmituns.

There was a subdued little group of occupants when I was there; Mr. Morse, the American pill-maker, Mr. Williams, another American, an ex-Portuguese Minister and his wife and son (exiles these from Portugal), a little Dutch Baroness who was said to be a great friend of Gyp's, half a dozen English nurses and two wounded German officers.

I made friends quickly with the nurses and the Americans, and to look into English eyes again gave me a peculiarly soothing sense of relief that taught me (if I needed teaching) how alone I was in all these dangers and agitations.

Mr. Williams had a queer experience. I have often wondered why America did not resent it on his account.

He was arrested and taken prisoner for talking about the horrors of Louvain in a train. He was released while I was there. I saw him dashing into the hotel one evening, a brown paper parcel under his arm. There was quite a little scene in the waiting-room; everyone came round him asking what had happened. It seemed that as he stepped out of the tram he was confronted by German officers, who promptly conducted him into a "detention honorable."

There he was stripped and searched, and in the meanwhile private detectives visited his room at the Metropole and went through al his belongings.

Nothing of a compromising nature being found, Mr. Williams was allowed to go free after twenty-four hours, having first to give his word that in future he would not express himself in public.

When I invited him to describe to me what happened in his "detention honorable," he answered with a strained smile, "No more talking for me!"

Surely this insult to a free-born American must have been a bitter dose for the American Consulate to swallow.

But perhaps they were too busy to notice it!

When I called at the Consulate the place was crowded with English nurses begging to be helped away from Brussels. I found that Mr. Richards had already put in a word on my behalf.

This is what they gave me at the American Consulate in Brussels as a safeguard against the Germans. I shouldn't have cared to show it to the enemy! It seemed to me to deliver me straight into their hands. I hid it in the lining of my hat with my passport.

CHAPTER XXIII

CHANSON TRISTE

Chilly and wet to-day in Brussels.

And oh, so triste, so triste!

Never before have I known a sadness like to this.

Not in cemetery, not in ruined town, not among wounded, coming broken from the battle, as on that red day at Hyst-op-Den-Berg.

A brooding soul – mist is in the air of Brussels. It creeps, it creeps. It gets into the bones, into the brain, into the heart. Even when one laughs one feels the ghostly visitant. All the joy has gone from life. The vision is clouded. To look at anything you must see Germans first.

Oh, horrible, horrible it is!

And hourly it grows more horrible.

Its very quietness takes on some clammy quality associated with graves.

Movement and life go on all round. People walk, talk, eat, drink, take the trams, shop. But all the while the Germans are there, the Germans are in their hotels, their houses, their palaces, their public buildings, Town Hall, Post Office, Palais de Justice, in their trams, in their cafés, in their restaurants –

At last I find a simile.

It is like being at home, in one's beloved home with one's beloved family all around one, and every room full *of cockroaches!*

CHAPTER XXIV

THE CULT OF THE BRUTE

Repellant, unforgettable, was the spectacle of the Germans strutting and posing on the steps of the beautiful Palais de Justice.

So ill did they fit the beauty of their background, that all the artist in one writhed with pain. Like some horrible vandal attempt at decoration upon pure and flawless architecture these coarse, brutish figures stood with legs apart, their flat round caps upon their solemn yokel faces giving them the aspect of a body of convicts, while behind them reared those noble pillars, yellow and dreamlike, suffering in horror, but with chaste dignity, the polluting nearness of the Hun.

The more one studies Hun physiognomy and physique, the more predominant grow those first impressions of the Cult of the Brute. Brutish is the clear blue eye, with the burning excited brain revealing itself in flashes such as one might see in the eye of a rhinoceros on the attack. Brutish is the head, so round and close cropped, resembling no other animal save German. Brutish are the ears flapping out so redly. The thick necks and incredibly thick legs have the tenacious look of elephants.

And oh, their little ways, their little ways!

In the Salle Du Tribunal de Commerce they put up clothes-lines, and hung their shirts and handkerchiefs there, while a bucket stood in the middle of the beautiful tesselated floor. And then, in exquisite taste, to give the Belgians a treat, this interior has been photographed and forced into an extraordinary little newspaper published in Brussels, printed in French but secretly controlled by the Germans, who splatter it with their photographs in every conceivable (and inconceivable) style.

And so we see them in their kitchen installed at the foot of the Monument, wearing aprons over their middle-aged tummies, blucher boots, and round flat caps. A pretty picture that!

They posed themselves for it; alone they did it. And this is how. They tipped up a big basket, and let it lie in the foreground on its side. Two Germans seized a table, lifting it off the ground. One man seated himself on a wooden bench with a tin of kerosene. Half a dozen others leaned up against the portable stoves, with folded arms, looking as if they were going to burst into Moody and Sankey hymns. All food, all bottles, were hidden. The dustbin was brought forward instead. And then the photographer said "gut!" And there they were! It was the Hunnish idea of a superb photograph of Army Cooks. Contrast it with Tommy's! How do you see Tommy when a war photographer gets him? His first thought is for an effect of "Cheer-oh!" He doesn't hide bottles and glasses. He brings them out, and lets you look at them. He doesn't, in the act of being photographed, lift a table. He lifts a tea-pot or a bottle if he has one handy. Give us Tommy all the time. Yes. All the time!

Another photograph shews the Huns in the Auditoire of the Cour de Cassation! More funny effects! They've brought forward all their knapsacks, and piled them on a desk for decoration. They themselves lie on the carpeted steps at full length. But they don't lounge. They can't. No man can lounge who doesn't know what to do with his hands. And Germans never know what to do with theirs.

When I saw that picture, showing the Hun idea of how a photograph should be taken, I felt a suffocation in my larynx. Then there was a gem called Un Coin de la Cour de Cassation. This shewed dried fish and sausages hanging on an easel! cheeses on the floor; and washing on the clothes-line.

And opposite this, on the other page was a photo of General Leman and his now famous letters to King Albert, the most touching human documents that were ever written to a King.

Sire,

Après des combats honorables livrés les 4, 5, et 6 aout par la 3me division d'armee renforcee, a partir du 5, par la 15me brigade, j'ai estimé que les forts de Liége ne pouvaient plus jouer que le rôle de forts d'arrêt. J'ai néanmoins conservé le gouvernement militaire de la place afin d'en coordonner la défense autant qu'il m'etait possible et afin d'exercer une action morale sur les garnisons des forts.

Le bien-fondé de ces resolutions à reçu par la suite des preuves sérieuses.

Votre Majeste n'ignore du reste pas que je m'etais installe au fort de Loncin, a partir du 6 août, vers midi.

Sire,

Vous apprendrez avec douleur que ce fort a sauté bier à 17 h. 20 environ, ensevelissant sous ses ruines la majeure partie de la garnison, peut-être les huit-dixièmes.

Si je n'ai pas perdu la vie dans cette catastrophe, c'est parce que mon escorte, composée comme suit: captaine commandant Collard, un sous-officier d'infanterie, qui n'a sans doute pas survecu, le gendarme Thevénin et mes deux ordonnances (Ch. Vandenbossche et Jos. Lecocq) m'a tiré d'un endroit du fort ou j'allais être asphyxié par les gaz de la poudre. J'ai été porte dans le fossé où je suis tombé. Un captaine allemand, du nom de Gruson, m'a donne à boire, mais j'ai été fait prisonnier, puis emmené à Liége dans une ambulance.

Je suis certain d'avoir soutenu l'honneur de nos armes. Je n'ai rendu ni la forteresse, ni les forts.

Daignez me pardonner, Sire, la negligeance de cette lettre je suis physiquement très abimé par l'explosion de Loncin.

En Allemagne, où je vais être dirigé, mes pensées seront ce qu'elles ont toujours été: la Belgique et son Roi. J'aurais volontiers donné ma vie pour les mieux servir, mais la mort n'a pas voulu de moi.

G. Leman.

CHAPTER XXV

DEATH IN LIFE

What is it I've been saying about gaiety?

How could one ever use such a word?

Here in the heart of Brussels one cannot recall even a memory of what it was like to be joyful!

I am in a city under German occupation; and I see around me death in life, and life in death. I see men, women, and children, with eyes that are looking into tombs. Oh those eyes, those eyes! Ah, here is the agony of Belgium – here in this fair white capital set like a snowflake on her hillside. Here is grief concentrated and dread accumulated, and the days go by, and the weeks come and pass, and then months – *then months!* – and still the agony endures, the Germans remain, the Belgians wake to fresh morrows, with that weight that is more bitter and heavier than Death, flinging itself upon their weary shoulders the moment they return to consciousness.

Yes. Waking in Brussels is grim as waking on the morn of execution!

Out of sleep, with its mercy of dream and forgetfulness, the *Bruxellois* comes back each morning to a sense of brooding tragedy. Swiftly this deepens into realization. The Germans are here. They are still here. The day must be gone through, the sad long day. There is no escaping it. The Belgian must see the grey figures striding through his beloved streets, shopping in his shops, walking and motoring in his parks and squares. He must meet the murderers in his churches, in his cafes. He must hear their laughter in his ears, and their loud arrogant speech. He must see them in possession of his Post Offices, his Banks, his Museums, his Libraries, his Theatres, his Palaces, his Hotels.

He must remain in ignorance of the world outside. Worst of all! When his poor tortured thoughts turn to one thought of his Deliverance, he must confront a terror sharper than all the rest. Then, he sees in clear vision, the ghastly fate that may fall upon the unarmed Brussels population the day the Germans are driven out. The whole beautiful city may be in flames, the whole population murdered. There is no one who can stop the Germans if they decide to ruin Brussels before evacuating it. One can only trust in their common-sense – and their mercy!

And at thought of mercy the *Bruxellois* gazes away down the flat, dusty road – away towards Louvain!

The peasants are going backwards and forwards to Louvain.

Little carts, filled with beshawled women and children, keep trundling along the road. A mud-splashed rickety waggonette is drawn up in front of a third-rate café. "Louvain" is marked on it in white chalk. On a black board, in the café window, is a notice that the waggonette will start when full. The day is desperately wet. There is a canvas roof to the waggonette, but the rain dashes through, sideways, and backwards and forwards. Under cover of the rain as it were, I step into the waggonette, and seat myself quietly among a group of peasants. Two more get in shortly after. Then off we start. In silence, all crouching together, we drive through the city, out through the northern gateway; soon we are galloping along the drear flat country-road that leads to the greatest tragedy of the War. It is ten o'clock when we start. At half-past eleven we are in Louvain. On the way we meet only peasants and little shop-keepers going to and from Brussels.

Over the flat bare country, through the grey atmosphere comes an impression of whiteness. My heart beats suffocatingly as I climb out of the waggonette and stand in the narrow Rue de la Station, looking along the tram-line. The heaps of debris nearly meet across the street.

The rain is falling in Louvain; it beats through the ruined spaces; it does its best to wash out the blood-stains of those terrific days in August. And the people, oh, the brave people. They are actually making a pretence of life. A few shops are opened, a cafe opposite the ruined theatre is full of pale, trembling old men, sipping their byhr or coffee; Louvain is just alive enough to whisper the word *"Death!"*

But with that word it whispers also "Immortality."

In its ruin Louvain seems to me to have taken on a beauty that could never have belonged to it in other days. Those great fair buildings with gaps in their sides, speak now with a voice that the whole world listens to. The Germans have smashed and flattened them, burnt and destroyed them. But the glory of immortality that Death alone can confer rests upon them now. Out of those ruins has sprung the strongest factor in the War. Louvain, despoiled and desolate, has had given into her keeping the greatest power at work against Germany. Louvain, in her waste and mourning, has caused the world to pause and think. She has made hearts bleed that were cold before; she has opened the world's eyes to Germany's brutality!

Actually, in Africa, Louvain it was that decided a terribly critical situation. Because of Louvain, many, many hesitating partisans of Germany threw in their cause with the Allies.

Ah, Louvain! Take heart! In your destruction you are indestructible. You faced your day of carnage. Your civilians bravely opposed the enemy. It was all written down in Destiny's white book. The priests that were shot in your streets, the innocent women and children who were butchered, they have all achieved great things for Belgium, and they will achieve still greater things yet.

Louvain, proud glorious Louvain, it is because of you that Germany can never win. Your ruins stand for Germany's destruction. It is not you who are ruined. It is Germany!

* * * *

I wander about. I am utterly indifferent to-day. If a German officer took it in his head to suspect me I would not care. Such is my state of mind wandering among the ruins of Louvain.

I am surprised to find that in the actual matter of ruins Louvain is less destroyed than I expected.

Compared with Aerschot, the town has not been as ruthlessly destroyed. Aerschot no longer exists. Louvain is still here. Among the ruined monuments, houses and shops are occupied. An attempt at business goes on. The heaps of masonry in the streets are being cleared away. With her interior torn out, the old theatre still stands upright. The train runs in and out among the ruins.

The University is like a beautiful skeleton, with the wind and rain dashing through the interstices between her white frail bones.

Where there are walls intact, and even over the ruins, the Germans have pasted their proclamations.

Veuve D. for insulting an official was sentenced to ten years in prison.

Jean D. for opposing an official, was shot.

And in flaunting placards the Germans beg the citizens of Louvain to understand that they will meet with nothing but kindness and consideration from Das Deutsche Heer, as long as they behave themselves.

I step into a little shop as a motor car full of German officers dashes by.

"How brave you are to keep on," I say to the little old woman behind the counter. "It must be terribly sad and difficult."

"If we had more salt," she says, "we shouldn't mind! But one must have salt. And there is none left in Louvain. We go to Brussels for it, but it grows more and more difficult to obtain, even there."

"And food?"

"Oh, the English will never let us starve," she says. "Mon Mari, he says so, and he knows. He was in England forty years ago. He was in the household of Baron D., the Belgian Ambassador in London. Would you like to see Mon Mari."

I went into the room behind the shop.

Mon Mari was sitting in a big chair by the window, looking out over some rain-drenched purple cabbages.

He was a little old Belgian, shrivelled and trembling. He had been shot in the thigh on that appalling August day when Louvain attempted to defend herself against the murderers. He was lame, broken, useless, aged. But his sense of humour survived. It flamed up till I felt a red glow in that chilly room looking over the rain-wet cabbages, and laughter warmed us all three among the ruins, myself, and the little old woman, and Mon Mari.

"Yesterday," he said, "an American Consul was coming in my shop. He was walking with a German Colonel. The American says: 'How could you Germans destroy a beautiful city like Louvain?' And the Alboche answered, 'We didn't know it was beautiful!' "

And the old woman echoes ponderingly:

"Didn't know it was beautiful!"

CHAPTER XXVI

THE RETURN FROM BRUSSELS

From Brussels to Ninove, from Ninove to Sottegem, from Sottegem to Ghent, from Ghent to Antwerp; that was how I got back!

At the outskirts of Brussels, on a certain windy corner, I stood, waiting my chance of a vehicle going towards Ghent.

The train-lines were still cut, and the only way of getting out of Brussels was to drive, unless one went on foot.

At the windy corner, accompanied by Jean and his two sisters, I stood, watching a wonderful drama.

There were people creeping in, as well as creeping out, peasants on foot, women and children who had fled in terror and were now returning to their little homes. It seemed to me as if the Germans must purposely have left this corner unwatched, unhindered, probably in the hope of getting more and more to return.

Little carts and big carts clattered up and came to a standstill alongside an old white inn, and Jean bargained and argued on my behalf for a seat.

There was one tiny cart, drawn by a donkey, with five young men in it.

The driver wanted six passengers, and began appealing to me in Flemish to come in.

"I will drive you all the way to Ghent if you like," he said.

"How much?"

"Ten francs."

Suddenly a hand pulled at my sleeve, and a hoarse voice whispered in my ear:

"Non, non, Madam. You mustn't go with them. Don't you know who they are?"

It was a rough-faced little peasant, and his blue eyes were full of distress.

I felt startled and impressed, and wondered if the five young men were murderers.

"They are the Newspaper Sellers!" muttered the blue-eyed peasant under his breath.

If he had said they were madmen his tone could not have been more awestruck.

After a while I found a little cart with two seats facing each other, two hard wooden seats. One bony horse stood in the shafts. But I liked the look of the three Belgian women who were getting in, and one of them had a wee baby. That decided me. I felt that the terrors of the long drive before me would be curiously lightened by that baby's presence. Its very tininess seemed to make things easier. Its little indifferent sleeping face, soft and calm and fragrant among its white wool dainties, seemed to give the lie to dread and terror; seemed to hearten one swiftly and sweetly, seemed to say: "Look at me, I'm only a month old. But I'm not frightened of anything!"

And now I must say good-bye to Jean, and good-bye to his two plump young sisters.

They are the dearest friends I have in the world – or so it seems to me as I bid them good-bye.

"Bonne chance, Madam!" they whisper.

I should like to have kissed Jean, but I kissed the sisters instead, then feeling as if I were being cut in halves, I climbed, lonely and full of sinister dread, into the little cart, and the driver cracked his whip, shouting, "Allons, Fritz!" to his bony horse and off we started, a party of eight all told. The three Belgian women sat opposite me; two middle-aged men were beside me, and the driver and another man were on the front seat.

Hour after hour we drove, hour after hour there was no sun. The

land looked flat and melancholy under this grey sky, and we were at
our old game now.

"Have you seen the Germans?"

"Yes, yes, the Germans are there," pointing to the right.

And we would turn to the left, tacking like a boat in the storm.
Terrific firing was going on. But the baby, whose name the mother
told me was Solange, slept profoundly, the three women chattered
like parrots, and the driver shouted incessantly, "Allons, Fritz, allez-
Komm!" and Fritz, throwing back his head, plodded bravely on,
dragging his heavy load with a superb nonchalance that led him into
cantering up the hills, and breaking into gallops when he got on the
flat road again. Hour after hour Fritz cantered, and galloped and trot-
ted, dragging eight people along as though they were so many pods.

Ce 10. 12. 14.

MADAME CREED,

Le passage à Londres, je me permets de me rappeler à votre bon sou-
venir. En effet, rappelez-vous votre retour de Bruxelles, en octobre
dernier: dans la carriole se trouvaient 2 messieurs et 3 dames (l'une avec
un bébé que vous avez tenu dans les bras) dont 2 institutrices. Y'en suis
une des deux, Mme. Stoefs. Y'ai éte à Gand espérant vous revoir, mais
vous étiez repartie dejà Peut, être ici a Londres, amai-je ce plaisir. Y'y
suis encore jusqu a la fin de cette semaine, done soyez assez aimable de
me dire oú et quand nous puorrions nous rencontrer. Voici mon adresse:
Mme. Stoefs: Verstegen, 53, Maple Street, W. An plaisir de vous revoir,
je vous présente mes cordiales salutations.

CHARLOTTE STOEFS.
Institutrice a Bruxelles.

One bleak December day in London there came to me this letter,

and by it alone I know that Fritz and the baby Solange, and the eight
of us are no myth, no figment of my imagination. We really did, all
together, drive all day long through the German-infected country, to
east, to west, to north, to south, through fields and byways, and
strange little villages, over hills and along valleys, with the cannon
always booming, the baby always sleeping and old Fritz always going
merry and bright.

By noon, we might have known each other a thousand years. I had
the baby on my knee, the three men cracked walnuts for us all, and
everyone talked at once; strange talk, the strangest in all the world.

"So they killed the priest!"

"She hid for two days in the water-closet."

"She doesn't know what has happened to her five children."

"They were stood in a row and every third one was *fusillé*."

"They found his body in the garden!"

"Il est tout-a-fait ruine."

Then suddenly one of the ladies, who knew a little English, said
with a friendly smile:

"I have liked very much the English novel – how do you call it
something about a lamp. Everyone reads it. It is our favourite English
book. It is splendid. We read it in French too."

And every now and then for hours she and I would try guessing the
name of that something-about-a-lamp book. But we never got it. It
was weeks later when I remembered "The Lamplighter."[8]

At last we crossed the border from Brabant into Flanders, and galloping up a long hill we found ourselves in Ninove. It was in a terrific state of excitement. Here we saw the results of the fighting I had
heard at Enghien on the Saturday. The Germans had pillaged and
destroyed. Houses lay tumbled on the streets, the peasants stood
grouped in terror, the air was full of the smell of burning. At a house
where we bought some apples we saw a sitting-room after the Huns

---

[8] *The Lamplighter* by Maria Susanna Cummins, first published in 1854.

had finished it. Every bit of glass and china in the room was smashed, tumblers, wine-glasses, jugs, plates, cups, saucers lay in heaps all over the floor. All the pictures were cut from the frames, all the chairs and tables were broken to bits. The cushions were torn open, the book-shelves toppled forward, the books lay dripping wet on the grey carpet as if buckets of water had been poured over them. Jam tins, sardine tins, rubbish and filth were all over the carpet, and bottles were everywhere. It was a low, degrading sight.

CHAPTER XXVII

"THE ENGLISH ARE COMING"

I am back in Antwerp and the unexpected has happened.

We are besieged.

The siege began on Thursday.

The mental excitement of these last days passes all description.

And yet Antwerp is calm outwardly, and but for the crowds of peasants, pouring into the city with their cows and their bundles, one would hardly know that the Germans were really attacking us at last.

The Government has issued an order that anyone who likes may leave Antwerp; but once having done so no one will be permitted to return; and that quite decides us; we will remain.

All day long the cannon are booming and pounding; sometimes they sound so near that one imagines a shell must have burst in Antwerp itself; and sometimes they grow fainter, they are obviously receding.

Or so we tell ourselves hopefully.

We are always hopeful; we are always telling each other that things are going better.

Everyone is talking, talking, talking.

Everyone is asking, "What do you think? Have you heard any news?"

Everyone is saying, "But of course it will be all right!"

"The Germans have been driven back five kilometres," says one civilian.

"Have you heard the news? The Germans have been driven back six kilometres!" says another.

And again: "Have *you* heard the good news? Germans driven back seven kilometres!"

And at last a curious mental condition sets in.

We lose interest in the cannon, and we go about our business, just as if those noises were not ringing in our ears, even as we sit at dinner in our hotel.

There is one little notice pasted up about the hotel that, simply as it reads, fills one with a new and more active terror than shell-fire: – *"Il n'y a pas d'eau!"*

This is because the German shells have smashed the Waterworks at Wavre S. Catherine. And so, in the meantime, Antwerp's hotels are flooded with carbolic, and we drink only mineral waters, and wait (hopeful as ever) for the great day when the bathrooms will be opened again.

These nights are stiflingly hot. And the mosquitoes still linger. Indeed they are so bad sometimes that I put eucalyptus oil on my pillow to keep them away. How strange that all this terrific firing should not have frightened them off! I come to the conclusion that mosquitoes are deaf.

The curious thing is, no one can tell, by looking at Antwerp, that she is going through the greatest page in all her varied history. Her shops are open. People sit at crowded cafes sipping their coffee or beer. A magnificent calm prevails. There is no sense of active danger. The lights go out at seven instead of eight. By ten o'clock the city is asleep, save for the coming and going of clattering troops over the rough-flagged streets and avenues. Grapes and pears and peaches are displayed in luxuriant profusion, at extraordinarily low prices. Fish and meat are dearer, but chickens are still very cheap. The *"Anversois"* still take as much trouble over their cooking, which is uncommonly good, even for Belgium.

And then on Saturday, with the sharpness and suddenness of lightning, the terrible rumour goes round that Antwerp is going to *surrender*, – yes, surrender – rather than run the risk of being destroyed like

Louvain, and Termonde, and Aerschot.

The Legation has received orders that the Government is about to be moved to Ostend. Crowds of people begin to hurry out of Antwerp in motor cars, until the city looks somewhat like London on a Sunday afternoon, half-empty, and full of bare spaces, instead of crowded and animated as Antwerp has been ever since the Government moved here from Brussels.

And then, on Sunday, comes a change.

The news spreads like wild-fire that the Legations have had their orders countermanded early in the morning.

They are to wait further instructions.

Something has happened. *THE ENGLISH ARE COMING!*

CHAPTER XXVIII

MONDAY

A golden, laughing day is this 5th of October.

As I fly along in my car I soon sense a new current, vivid and electric, flowing along with the stream of Belgian life.

Oh, the change in the sad, hollow-eyed Belgian officers and men! They felt that help was coming at last. All this time they had fought alone, unaided. There was no one who could come to them, no one free to help them. And the weeks passed into months, and Liege, and Louvain, and Brussels, and Aerschot, and Namur, and Malines, and Termonde have all fallen, one by one. And high hopes have been blighted, and the enemy in its terrific strength has swept on and on, held back continually by the ardour and valour of the little Belgian Army which is still indomitable at heart, but tired, very tired. Haggard, hollow-eyed, exhausted, craving the rest they may not have, these glorious heroes revive as if by magic under the knowledge that other troops are coming to help theirs in this gargantuan struggle for Antwerp. The yellow khaki seems to sweep along with the blue uniforms like sunlight. But the gentle-faced, slow-speaking English are humble and modest enough, God knows!

"It's the high-explosive shells that we mind most," says a Belgian Lieutenant to an English Tommy.

"P'raps we'll mind them too," says Tommy humbly. "We ain't seen them yet!"

At the War Office, Count Chabeau has given me a special permit to go to Lierre.

Out past Mortsell, I notice a Belgian lady standing among a crowd of soldiers. She wears black. Her dress is elegant, yet simple. I admire her furs, and I wonder what on earth she is doing here, right out in the middle of the fortifications, far from the city. Belgian ladies are seldom seen in these specified zones.

Suddenly her eyes meet mine, and she comes towards me, drawn by the knowledge that we are both women.

She leans in at my car window. And then she tells me her story, and I learn why she looks so pale and worried.

Just down the road, a little further on, in the region in which we may not pass, is her villa, which has been suddenly requisitioned by the English. All in a hurry yesterday, Madame packed up, and hurried away to Antwerp, to arrange for her stay there. This morning she has returned to fetch her dogs.

But voilà! She reaches this point and is stopped. The way is blocked. She must not go on. No one can pass without a special laisser-passer; which she hasn't got.

So here, hour after hour, since six o'clock in the morning, she stands, waiting pitifully for a chance to get back to her villa and take away her dogs, that she fears may be starving.

"Mes pauvre chiens!" she keeps exclaiming.

And now a motor car approaches from the direction of Lierre, with an English officer sitting beside the chauffeur.

I tell him the story of the dogs and ask what can be done.

The officer does not reply.

He almost looks as if he has not heard.

His calm, cool face shows little sign of anything at all.

He merely turns his car round and flashes away along the white tree-shadowed and cannon-lined road that he has just traversed.

Ten minutes go by, then another ten.

Then back along the road flashes the grey car.

And there again is Colonel Farquharson, cool, calm, and unperturbed.

And behind him, in the car, barking joyfully at the sight of their mistress, are three big dogs.

"Mais comme les Anglais sont gentils!" say the Belgian soldiers along the road.

* * * *

Out of the burning town of Lierre that same day a canary and a grey Congo parrot are tenderly handed over to my care by a couple of English Tommies who have found them in a burning house.

The canary is in a little red cage, and the Tommies have managed to put in some lumps of sugar.

"The poor little thing is starving!" says a Tommy compassionately. "It'll be better with you, ma'am."

I bring the birds back in my car to Antwerp.

But the parrot is very frightened.

He will not eat. He will not drink. He looks as if he is going to die, until I ask Mr. Cherry Kearton to come and see him. And then, voilà! The famous English naturalist bends over him, talks, pets him, and in a few minutes "Coco" is busy trimming Cherry Kearton's moustache with his little black beak, and from that very moment the bird begins to recover.

As I write the parrot and canary sit here on my table, the parrot perching on the canary's cage.

The boom of cannon is growing fainter and fainter as the Germans appear to be pushed further and further back; the canary is singing, and the grey parrot is cracking nuts; and I think of the man who rescued them, and hope that all goes well with him, who, with death staring him in the face, had time and thought to save the lives of a couple of birds. His name he told me was Sergeant Thomas Marshall of Winston Churchill's Marines.

He said: "If you see my wife ever, you can tell her you've met me, ma'am."

CHAPTER XXIX

TUESDAY

It is Tuesday now. At seven o'clock in the morning old sad-eyed Maria knocks at my door.

"Good news, Madame! Malines has been retaken!"

That is cheering. And old Maria and myself, like everyone else, are eager to believe the best.

The grey day, however, is indescribably sombre.

From a high, grassy terrace at the top of the hotel I look out across the city towards the points where the Germans are attacking us. Great black clouds that yet are full of garish light float across the city, and through the clouds one, two, three, four aeroplanes can be seen, black as birds, and moving continually hither and thither, while far below the old town lies, with its towers and gilded Gothic beauty, and its dark red roofs, and its wide river running to meet the sea.

I go down to the War Office and see Commandant Chabeau. He looks pale and haggard. His handsome grey eyes are full of infinite sadness.

"To-day it would be wiser, Madame, that you don't go out of the city," he says in his gentle, chivalrous voice. "C'est trop dangereux! "

I want to ask him a thousand questions.

I ask him nothing, I go away, back to the hotel.

One o'clock, and we learn that the fighting outside is terribly hot.

Two o'clock.

Cars come flying in.

They tell us that shells are falling about five miles out, on Vieux

Dieux.

Three o'clock.

A man rushes in and says that all is over; the last train leaves Antwerp to-night; the Government is going; it is our last chance to escape.

"How far is Holland?" asks someone.

"About half an hour away," he answers.

I listen dreamily. Holland sounds very near. I wonder what I am going to do. Am I going to stay and see the Germans enter? But maybe they will never enter. The unexpected will happen. We shall be saved at the eleventh hour. It is impossible that Antwerp can fall.

"They will be shelling the town before twenty-four hours," says one young man, and he calls for another drink. When he has had it he says he wishes he hadn't.

"They will never shell the town," says a choleric old Englishman. And he adds in the best English manner, "It could never be permitted!"

Outside, the day dies down.

The sound of cannon has entirely ceased.

One can hear nothing now, nothing at all, but the loud and shrill cries of the newsboys and women selling *Le Matin d'Anvers* and *Le Métropole* in the streets.

A strange hushed silence hangs over the besieged city, and through the silence the clocks strike six, and almost immediately the *maître d'hôtel* comes along and informs us that we ought to come in to dinner soon, as to-day the lights must go out at nightfall!

But I go into the streets instead.

It seems to me that the population of Antwerp has suddenly turned into peasants.

Peasants everywhere, in crowds, in groups, in isolated numbers. Bareheaded women, hollow-cheeked men, little girls and boys, and all with bundles, some pathetically small, done up in white or blue cloths, and some huge and grotesque, under which the peasants stagger along through the streets that were fashionable streets only just now, and now have turned into a sort of sad travesty of the streets of some distant village.

A curious rosy hue. falls over the faces in the streets, the shop-windows glow like rubies, the gold on the Gothic buildings burns like crimson fire.

Overhead a magnificent sunset is spreading its banners out over the deserted city.

Then night falls; the red fades; Antwerp turns grey and sombre.

But the memory of that rose in the west remains, and in hope we wait, we are still waiting, knowing not what the morrow may bring forth.

CHAPTER XXX

WEDNESDAY

Last night the moon was so bright that my two pets, rescued from the ruins of Lierre, woke up and began to talk.

Or was it the big guns that woke them, the canary, and the grey Congo parrot?

It might have been!

For sometimes the city seemed to shake all over, and as I lay in bed I wondered who was firing: Germans, Belgians, English, which?

About three o'clock, between dozing and listening to the cannon, I heard a new sound, a strange sound, something so awful that I almost felt my hair creep with horror.

It was a man crying in the room under mine.

Through the blackness of the hour before dawn a cry came stealing: *"Mon fils! Mon fils!"*

Out of the night it came, that sudden terrific revelation of what is going on everywhere beneath the outward calm of this nation of heroes.

And one had not realised it because one had seen so few tears.

One had almost failed to understand, in the outer calm of the Belgians, what agony went on beneath.

And now, in the midnight, the veil is torn aside, and I see a human heart in extremis, writhing with agony, groaning as the wounded never groan, stricken, bleeding, prostrate, overwhelmed with the enormity of its sorrow.

"Mon fils! Mon fils!"

Since I heard that old man weeping I want to creep to the feet of Christ and the Mother of Christ, and implore Their healing for these poor innocent broken hearts, trodden under the brutal feet of another race of human beings.

* * * *

At four, unable to sleep, I rose and dressed and went downstairs.

In the dim, unswept palm court I saw a bearded man with two umbrellas walking feverishly up and down, while the sleepy night porter leaned against a pillar yawning, watching for the cab that the *chass* had gone to look for. It came at last, and the bearded gentleman, with a sigh, stepped in, and drove away into the dusky dawn, a look of unutterable sadness seeming to cloak his face and form as he disappeared.

"*Il est triste, ce monsieur là*" commented our voluble little Flemish porter. "He is a Minister of the Government, and he must leave Antwerp, he must depart for Ostend. His boat leaves at five o'clock this morning."

"So the Government is really moving out," I think to myself mechanically.

A little boy runs in from the chill dawn-lit streets.

It is only half-past four, but a Flemish paper has just come out. – *Het Laatste Nieuwy.*

The boy throws it on the table where I sit writing to my sister in England, who is anxious for my safety.

I struggle to find out what message lies behind those queer Flemish words.

De Toestand Te Antwerpen Is Zeer Ernstig.

What does it mean?

Zeer Ernstig?

Is it good? Is it bad? I don't know the word.

I call to the night porter, and he comes out and translates to me, and as I glean the significance of the news I admire that peasant boy's calm.

"*La situation a Anvers est grave*" he says. "The Burgomaster announces to the population that the bombardment of Antwerp and its environs is imminent. It is understood, of course" (translating literally), "that neither the threat nor the actual bombardment will have any effect on the strength of our resistance, which will continue to the very last extremity!"

So we know the worst now.

Antwerp is not to hand herself over to the Germans. She is going to fight to the death. Well, we are glad of it! We know it is the only thing she could have done!

* * * *

And now the hotel wakes right up, and dozens of sleepy, worn, hollow-cheeked officers and soldiers in dirty boots come down the red-carpeted stairs clamouring for their *café-au-lait*.

The morning is very cold, and they shiver sometimes, but they are better after the coffee and I watch them all go off smoking cigarettes.

Poor souls! Poor souls!

After the coffee, smoking cigarettes, they hurry away, to...

The day is past sunrise now, and floods of golden light stream over the city, where already great crowds are moving backwards and forwards.

Cabs drive up continually to the great railway station opposite with piles of luggage, and I think dreamily how very like they are to London four-wheelers, taking the family away to the seaside!

And still the city remains marvellously calm, in spite of the ever-increasing movements. People are going away in hundreds, in thousands. But they are going quietly, calmly. Processions of black-robed nuns file along the avenues under the fading trees. Long lines of Belgian cyclists flash by in an opposite direction in their gay yellow and green uniforms. The blue and red of the French and English banners never looked brighter as the wind plays with them, and the sunlight sparkles on them, while the great black and red and gold Belgian flags lend that curious note of sombre dignity to the crowded streets.

But not a word of regret from anyone. That is the Belgian way.

Belgians all, to-day I kneel at your feet.

Oh God, what those people are going through!

God, what they are suffering and to suffer! How can they bear it? Where do they get their heroism?   Is it – it must be – from Above!

CHAPTER XXXI

THE CITY IS SHELLED

That day, seated in wicker chairs in the palm court, we held a counsel of war, all the War-Correspondents who were left. The question was whether the Hotel Terminus was not in too dangerous a position. Its extreme nearness to the great railway station made its shelling almost inevitable when the bombardment of the city began in earnest. We argued a lot. One suggested one hotel, one another. To be directly northward was clearly desirable, as the shells would come from southward.

Mr. Cherry Kearton, Mr. Cleary, and Mr. Marshall, decided on the Queen's Hotel, somewhere near the quay. Their point was that it would be easier to get away from there. Mr. Robinson and Mr. Phillips refused to change from the Terminus. Mr. Fox, Mr. Lucien Arthur Jones, and myself chose the Wagner, as being in the most northerly direction, the farthest away from the forts, and the nearest to the Breda Gate, which led to Holland. In the moonlight, after dinner, taking my canary with me, I moved to my new quarters, accompanied to the doors by that little band of Englishmen, Cherry Kearton carrying my parrot. It was then ten o'clock.

Strange things were to happen before we met again.

Precisely at eleven the first shell fell. Whiz! It fled in a fury across the sky and burst somewhere in the direction of the Cathedral. As it exploded I shut my eyes, clenched my hands, and sank on the floor by my bedside, saying to myself, "God, I'm dead!"

And I thought I was too.

The enormity of that sound-sensation seemed to belong to a transition from this world to the next. It scarcely seemed possible to pass through that noise and come out alive.

That was the first shell, and others followed quickly. The Hotel was alive immediately. Sleep was impossible. I crept down into the vestibule. It was all dark, save for one little light at the porter's door! I got a chair, drew it close to the light and sat down. I had a notebook and pencil, and to calm and control myself and not let my brain run riot I made notes of exactly what people said. I sat there all night long!

Every now and then the doors would burst open and men and women would rush in.

Once it was two slim, elegant ladies in black, with white fox stoles, who had run from their house because a shell had set fire to the house next door.

They came into the pitch-black vestibule, moving about by the little point of light made by their tiny electric torch. They asked for a room. There was none. So they asked to sit in the dark, empty restaurant, and as I saw them disappear into that black room where many refugees were already gathered, sleeping on chairs and floors and tables I could not help being amazed at the strangeness of it all, the unlikeness of it all to life, – these two gently-nurtured sisters with their gentle manners, their white furs, their electric light, gliding noiselessly along the burning, beshelled streets, and asking for a room in the first hotel they came to without a word about terror, and with expressions on their faces that utterly belied the looks of fright and terror that the stage has almost convinced us are the real thing.

Swing goes the door and in comes a man who asks the porter a question.

"Is Monsieur L. here?"

"Qui, Monsieur," replies the porter.

"Where is he?"

"He is in bed."

"Go to him and tell him that a shell has just fallen on the Bank of

Anvers. Tell him to rise and come out at once. He is a Bank Official
and he must come and help to save the papers before the bank is
burned down! Tell him Monsieur M., the Manager, came for him."

Swing, and the Bank Manager has gone through the door again out
into that black and red shrieking night.

Swing again, and three people hurry in, three Belgians, father,
mother and a little fair-haired girlie, whom they hold by each hand,
while the father cradles a big box of hard cash under one arm.

"The shells are falling all around our home!" they say.

The porter points to the restaurant door.

"Merci bien," and "Je vous remerci beaucoup," murmur father and
mother.

They vanish into the dark, unlit restaurant with its white table-
cloths making pale points athwart the stygian blackness of the huge
room.

Then an Englishman comes down the stairs behind me, flapping
his Burberry rainproof overcoat. He is a War-Correspondent.

"What a smell!" he says to the porter. "Is gas escaping somewhere?"

"No, sir," says the porter, pulling his black moustache.

He is very distrait and hardly gives the famous War-Correspondent
a thought.

"It *is* gas!" persists the War-Correspondent. "There must be a leak-
age somewhere."

He opens the door.

A horrible whiff of burning petroleum and smoke blows in, and a
Belgian soldier enters also.

"What's the smell?" asks the War-Correspondent.

"The Germans are dropping explosives on the city, trying to set fire
to it,"answers the Belgian.

"Good lor, I must have a look!" says the War-Correspondent.

He goes out.

Two wounded officers come down the stairs behind me.

"Bill, please, porter. How much? We must be off now to the forts!"

"Don't know the bill,"says the porter. "I'm new, the other man ran away. He didn't like shells. You can pay some other time, Messieurs!"

"Bien!" says the officers.

They swing their dark cloaks across their shoulders and pass out.

They come back no more, no, never any more.

Then an old, old man limps in on the arm of a young, ever-young Sister of Mercy.

"He is deaf and dumb," she says, "I found him and brought him here. He will be killed in the streets."

Her smile makes sunshine all over the blackness of that haunted hall; the mercy of it, the sweetness of it, the holiness are something one can never forget as, guiding the old man, she leads him into the dark restaurant and tends him through the night.

Then again the door swings open.

"The petroleum tanks have been set on fire by the Belgians themselves!" says a big man with a big moustache. "This is the end."

He is the proprietor himself.

And here up from the stairs behind us that lead down into the cellars, comes his wife, wrapped in furs.

"Henri, I heard your voice. I am going. I cannot stand it. I shall flee to Holland with little Marie. Put me into the motor car. My legs will not carry me. I fear for the child so much!"

A kiss, and she and little Marie flee away through the madness of the night towards the Breda Gate and the safety of some Dutch village across the border.

Every now and then I would open the swing-doors and fly like mad on tip-toe to the corner of the Avenue de Commerce, and there, casting one swift glance right and left, I would take in the awful panorama of scarlet flames. They were leaping now over the Marchée Aux Souliers, the street which corresponds with our Strand. While I watched I heard the shrieking rush of one shell after another, any one of which might of course well have fallen where I stood.

But I knew they wouldn't. I felt as safe and secure there in that shell-swept corner as if I had been a child again, at home in silent, sleepy, faraway Australia!

The fact is when you are in the midst of danger, with shells bursting round you, and the city on fire, and the Germans closing in on
you, and your friends and home many hundreds of miles away, your
brain works in an entirely different way from when you are living
safely in your peaceful Midlands.

Quite unconsciously, one's ego asserts itself in danger, until it seems
that one carries within one a world so important, so limitless, and
immortal, that it appears invincible before hurt or death.

This is an illusion, of course; but what a beautiful and merciful one!

When danger comes your way this illusion will begin to weave a
sort of fairy haze around you, making you feel that those shrieking
shells can never fall on you!

Seldom indeed while I was at the front did I hear anyone say, "I'm
afraid." How deeply and compassionately considerate Nature is to us
all! She has supplied us with a store of emotional glands, and fitted us
up with many a varying sensation, of which curiosity is the liveliest
and strongest. Then when it comes to a race between Fear and
Curiosity, in ninety-nine cases out of a hundred Curiosity wins hands
down. In real danger our curiosity, and our unconscious but deep-
seated belief in the ego, carry us right over the frightful terrors that
we imagine we should feel were we thinking the thing out quietly in
a safe land. *Then*, we tremble and shiver! *Then*, we remember the
word "Scream." *Then*, we understand the meaning of fear! *Then*, we
run (in our thoughts) into caves and cellars. But when the real thing
comes we put our heads out of the windows, we run out into the
streets, we go towards danger and not away from it, driven thither by
the mighty emotion of Curiosity, which, when all is said and done, is
one of the most delightful because the most electrifying of all human
sensations.

Is this brutal? Is it hard-hearted? Is it callous, indifferent, cruel? *No!*
For it bears no relation to our feelings for other people, *it only relates
to our own sensations about ourselves.* When a group of wounded
Belgians comes limping along, you look into their hollow, blackened
faces, you feel your heart break, and all your soul seems to dissolve in

one mighty longing to die for these people who have sacrificed their all for *you*; and you run to them, you help them all you can, you experience a passionate desire to give them everything you have, you turn out your pockets for them, you search for something, anything, that will help them.

No! You are not callous because you are curious! Quite the reverse, in fact. You are curious because you are alive, because you dwell in this one earth, and because you are created with the "sense" that you have a right to see and hear all the strange and wonderful things, all the terrors as well as all the glories that go to make up human existence.

Not to care, not to want to see, not to want to know, that is the callousness beyond redemption!

CHAPTER XXXII

THURSDAY

Thursday is a queer day, a day of no beginning and no ending.

It is haunted by such immense noise that it loses all likeness to what we know in ordinary life as "a day" – the thing that comes in between two nights.

It is, in fact, nothing but one cataclysmal bang and shriek of shells and shrapnel. The earth seems to break open from its centre every five minutes or so, and my brain begins to formulate to itself a tremendous sense of height and space, as well as of noise, until I feel as though I am in touch with the highest skies as well as with the lowest earth, because things that seem to belong essentially to earth are now happening in the skies.

The roof of the world is now enacting a rôle that is just as strange and just as surprising as if the roof of a theatre had suddenly begun to take part in a drama.

One looks above as often as one looks below or around one.

Flinging themselves forward with thin whinging cries like millions of mosquitoes on the attack, the shrapnel rushes perpetually overhead, and the high-explosive shells pour down upon the city, deafening, stupefying, until at last, by the very immensity of their noise, they gradually lose their power to affect one, even though they break all round.

Instead of listening to the bombardment I find myself listening crossly to the creaking of our lift, which makes noises exactly like those of the shrapnel outside.

In fact, when I am in my bedroom, and the lift is going up and down, I really don't know which is lift and which is shrapnel.

* * * *

Seven o'clock on Thursday morning.

The bombardment goes on fiercely, but I forget about it here in the big, bare, smoky cafe, because I cannot hear the lift.

A waiter brings me some coffee and I stand and drink it and look about me.

The café is surrounded with glass doors, and through these doors I see thousands and thousands of people hurrying for dear life along the roads.

As time goes on their numbers increase, until they are flowing by as steadily as some ceaseless black stream moving Holland-wards.

Men, women, children, nuns, priests, motor cars, carriages, cabs, carts, drays, trolleys, perambulators, every species of human being and of vehicle goes hurrying past the windows, and always the vehicles are laden to the very utmost with their freight of human life.

One's brain reels before the immensity of this thing that is happening here; a city is being evacuated by a million inhabitants; the city is in flames and shells are raining down on it; yet the cook is making soup in the kitchen...

Among the human beings struggling onwards towards the Breda Gate which will lead them to Holland, making strange little notes in the middle of the human beings, I see every now and then some poor pathetic animal, moving along in timid bewilderment – a sheep – a dog – a donkey – a cow – a horse – more cows perhaps than anything, big, simple, wondering cows, trudging along behind desolate little groups of peasants with all their little worldly belongings tied up in a big blue-and-white check handkerchief, while crash over their heads goes on the cannonading from the forts, and with each fresh shock the vast concourse of fleeing people starts and hurries forward.

It seems to me as though the End of the World will be very like to-day.

A huge gun-carriage, crowded with people, is passing. It is twenty feet long, and drawn by two great, bulky Flemish horses. Sitting all along the middle, with great wood stakes fixed along the edges to keep them from falling out, are different families getting away into Holland. Fathers, mothers, children. Two men go by with a clothes-basket covered with a blanket. Dozens of beautiful dogs, bereft of their collars in this final parting with their masters, run wildly back and forth along the roads. A boy with a bicycle is wheeling an old man on it. Three wounded blue and scarlet soldiers march along desolately, carrying brown paper parcels. Belgian Boy Scouts in khaki, with yellow handkerchiefs round their necks, flash past on bicycles. A man pushes a dog-cart with his three children and his wife in it, while the yellow dog trots along underneath, his tongue out. A black-robed priest rides by, mounted on a great chestnut mare, with a scarlet saddle cloth.

All the dramas of Æschylus pale into insignificance before this scene...

It is more than a procession of human beings. It is a procession of broken hearts, of torn, bleeding souls, and ruined homes, of desolate lives, of blighted hopes, and grim, grey despair–grim, grey despair in a thousand shapes and forms; and ever It hurries along the roads, ever It blocks the hotel windows, casting its thick shadows as the sun rises in the heavens, defying the black smoke palls that hang athwart the skies.

Sometimes I find tears streaming down my cheeks, and as they splash on my hands I look at them stupidly, and wonder what they are, and why they come, for no one can think clearly now.

Once it is the sight of a little, young, childlike nun, guarding an old, tottering, white-bearded man who is dumb as well as deaf, and who can only walk with short, little, halting steps.

Is she really going to try and get him to Holland, I wonder?

CHAPTER XXXIII

THE ENDLESS DAY

Years seem to have passed. Yet it is still Thursday morning, ten o'clock. The horror darkens.

We know the worst now. Antwerp is doomed. Nothing can save her, poor, beautiful, stately city that has seemed to us all so utterly impregnable all these months.

The evacuation goes on desperately, but the crowds fleeing northwards are diminishing visibly, because some five hundred thousands have already gone.

The great avenues, with their autumn-yellow trees and white, tall, splendid houses, grow bare and deserted.

Over the city creeps a terrible look, an aspect so poignant, so pathetic, that it reminds me of a dying soldier passing away in the flower of his youth.

The very walls of the high white houses, the very flags of the stony grey streets seem to know that Antwerp has fallen victim to a tragic fate; her men, women, and children must desert her; her homes must stand silent, cold and lonely, waiting for the enemy; her great hotels must be emptied; her shops and factories must put up their shutters; all the bright, gay, cheerful, optimistic life of this city that I have grown to love with an indescribable tenderness during the long weeks that I have spent within her fortified area is darkened now with despair.

Of the ultimate arrival of the Germans there is no longer any doubt, whether they take the town on a surrender, or by bombardment, or by assault.

I put on my hat and gloves, and go out into the streets. Oh, God! What a golden day!

Unbearable is the glitter of this sunlight shining over the agony of a nation!

CHAPTER XXXIV

I DECIDE TO STAY

For the moment the bombardment has ceased entirely. These little pauses are almost quaint in their preciseness.

One can count on them quite confidently not to be broken by stray shells.

And in the pause I am rushing along the Avenue de Commerce, trying to get round to the hotel where all my belongings are, when I run into three Englishmen with their arms full of bags, and overcoats, and umbrellas, and for a moment or two we stand there at the corner opposite the Gare Central all talking together breathlessly.

It was only last night at seven o'clock that we all dined together at the Terminus; but since then a million years have rolled over us; we have been snatched into one of History's most terrific pages; and we all have a burning breathless Saga of our own hanging on our lips, crying to be told aloud before the world.

We all fling out disjointed remarks, and I hear of the awful night in that quarter of the city.

"How are you going to get away?"

"And you, how are you going to get away?"

The tall, slight young man with the little dark moustache is Mr. Jeffries of the *Daily Mail*, who has been staying at the Hotel de l'Europe. With him is the popular Mr. Perry Robinson of the *Times*. The third is Mr. P. Phillips of the *Daily News*.

"I have just come from the Etat Majeur," Mr. Jeffries tells me hurriedly. "There is not a ghost of a hope now! Everyone has gone. We must get away at once."

"I am not going," I say. For suddenly the knowledge has come to me that I cannot leave the greatest of my dramas before the curtain rolls up in the last scene. In vain they argue, tell me I am mad. I am not going.

So they say good-bye and leave me.

CHAPTER XXXV

THE CITY SURRENDERS

Antwerp has surrendered!

It is Friday morning. All hope is over. The Germans are coming in at half-past one.

"Well," says Mr. Lucien Arthur Jones at last, at the end of a long discussion between him and Mr. Frank Fox and myself, "if you have really decided to stay, I'm going to give you this key! It belongs to the house of some wealthy Belgians who have fled to England. There is plenty of food and stores of all kind in the house. If need be, you might take shelter there!"

And he gave me the key and the address, and I, – luckily for myself, – I remembered it afterwards.

With a queer little choke in my throat, I stood on the hotel doorstep, watching those two Englishmen on their bicycles whirling away down the Avenue de Commerce.

In a moment they were swallowed up from my sight in the black pall of cloud and smoke that hung above the city, dropping from the leaden skies like long black fringes, arid hovering over the streets like thick funeral veils.

So they were gone!

The die was cast. I was alone now, all alone in the fated city.

At first, the thought was a little sickening.

But after a minute it gave me a certain amount of relief, as I realised that I could go ahead with my plans without causing anyone distress.

To feel that those two men had been worrying about my safety, and

were worrying still, was a very wretched sensation. They had enough
to think of on their own account! Somehow or other they had now
to get to a telegraph wire and send their newspapers in England the
story of Antwerp's fall, and the task before them was Herculean. The
nearest wires were in Holland, and they had nothing but their bicycles.

Turning back into the big, dim, deserted restaurant, I went to look
for the old patronne, whose black eyes dilated in her sad, old yellow
face at the sight of me in my dark blue suit, and white veil floating
from my little black hat.

"What, Madame! But they told me *les deux Anglais* have departed.
You have not gone with them?"

"Listen, Madame! I want you to help me. I am writing a book
about the War, and to see the Germans come into Antwerp is something I ought not to miss. I want to stay here!"

"Mais, c'est dangereux, Madame! Vous êtes Anglaise!"

"Well, I'm going to change that; I'm going to be Belgian. I want
you to let me pretend I'm a servant in your hotel. I'll put on a cap
and apron, and I'll do anything you like; then I'll be able to see things
for myself. It'll only be for a few hours. I'll get away this afternoon in
the motor. But I must see the incoming of the Germans first!"

The old woman seemed too bewildered to protest, and afterwards
I doubted if she had really understood me from the way she acted
later on.

Just at that moment Henri drove up in the motor, and came to a
standstill in front of the hotel.

The poor fellow looked more dead than alive. His pie-coloured face
was hollow, his lips were dry, his eyes standing out of his head. He
was so exhausted that he could scarcely step out of the car.

"I am sorry I am late," he groaned, "but it was impossible, impossible."

"You needn't worry about me, Henri," I whispered to him reassur-
ingly. "I'm not going to try to get out of Antwerp for several hours.
In fact, I am going to wait to see the Germans come in!"

Henri showed no surprise. There was no surprise left in him to show.

"Bon!" he said. "Because, to tell you the truth, Madame, I wouldn't go out of the city again just now. I couldn't do it. Getting to Holland, indeed," he went on, between gasps as he drank off one cup of coffee after another, "it's like trying to get through hell to get to Paradise... I've been seven hours driving about four miles there and back. It was horrible, it... was unbelievable... the roads are blocked so thick that there are no roads left. A million people are out there, struggling, fighting, and trying to get onwards, lying down on the earth fainting, dying."

And he suddenly sat down upon a chair, and fell fast asleep.

The sharp crack, crack of rifle fire woke him about five minutes later, and we all rushed to the door to see what was happening.

Oh, nerve-racking sight!

Across the grey square, through the grey-black morning, dogs were rushing, their tongues out.

The gendarmes pursuing them were shooting them down to save them the worse horrors of starvation that might befall them if they were left alive in the deserted city at the mercy of the Germans.

Madame X, a sad, distinguished-looking woman, a refugee from Lierre, whose house had been shelled, and who was destined to play a strange part in my story later on, now came over to us, and implored Henri to take her old mother in his car round to the hospital.

"She is eighty-four, *ma pauvre mère!* We tried to take her to Holland, but it was impossible. But now that the bombardment has ceased and the worst is over, it seems wiser to remain. In the hospital the mère will be surely safe! As for us, my husband and I, truly, we have lost our all. There is nothing left to fear!"

I offered to accompany the old lady to the hospital, and presently we started off. Henri and I, and the old wrinkled Flemish woman, and the buxom young Flemish servant, Jeanette.

We drove along the Avenue de Commerce, down the Avenue de

Kaiser, towards the hospital. The town was dead. Not a soul was to be seen. The Marché aux Souliers was all ablaze; I saw the Taverne Royale lying on the ground. Next to it was the Hotel de l'Europe, bomb-shattered and terrific in its ruins. I thought of Mr. Jeffries of the *Daily Mail* and shivered; that had been his hotel. The air reeked with petroleum and smoke. At last we got to the hospital.

The door-step was covered with blood, and red, wet blood was in drops and patches along the entrance.

As I went in, an unforgettable sight met my eyes.

I found myself in a great, dim ward, with the yellow, lurid skies looking in through its enormous windows, and its beds full of wounded and dying soldiers; and just as I entered, a white-robed Sister of Mercy was bending over a bed, giving the last unction to a dying man. Some brave *petit Belge*, who had shed his life-blood for his city, alas, in vain!

All the ordinary nurses had gone.

The Sisters of Mercy alone remained.

And suddenly it came to me like a strain of heavenly music that death held no terrors for these women; life had no fears.

Softly they moved about in their white robes, their benign faces shining with the look of the Cross.

In that supreme moment, after the hell of shot and shell, after the thousands of wounded and dead, after the endless agonies of attack and repulse and attack and defeat and surrender, something quite unexpected was here emerging, the essence of the Eternal Feminine, the woman supreme in her sheer womanhood; and like a bright bird rising from the ashes, the spirit of it went fluttering about that appalling ward.

The trained and untrained hospital nurses, devoted as they were, and splendid and useful beyond all words, had perforce fled from the city, either to accompany their escaping hospitals, or beset by quite natural fears of the Huns' brutality to their kind.

But the Sisters of Mercy had no fears.

The Cross stood between them and anything that might come to them.

And that was written in their faces, their shinings gentle faces...

Ah yes, the Priests and the half-forgotten Sisters of Mercy have indeed come back to their own in this greatest of all Wars!

Moving between the long lines of soldiers' beds I paused at the side of a little bomb-broken Belgian boy whose dark eyes opened suddenly to meet mine.

I think he must have been wandering, poor little child, and had come back with a start to life.

And seeing a face at his bedside he thought, perhaps, that I was German.

In a hoarse voice he gasped out, raising himself in terror:

"Je suis civil!"

Poor child, poor child!

The fright in his voice was heart-breaking. It said that if the *"Alboches"* took him for a *soldat*, they would shoot him, or carry him away into Germany...

I bent and kissed him.

"Je suis civil!"

He was not more than six years old.

* * * *

In another room of the hospital I found about forty children, little children varying from six months to five years. Some gentle nuns were playing with them.

"Les pauvres petites!" said one of the sisters compassionately. "They've all been lost, or left behind; there's no one to claim them, so we have brought them here to look after them."

And the baby gurgled and laughed, and gave a sudden leap in the sweet nun's arms.

Out of the hospital again, over the blood-stained doorstep, and back into the car.

There were a few devoted doctors and priests standing about in silence in the flower-wreathed passage entrance to the hospital. They were waiting for The End, waiting for the Germans to come in.

I can see them still, standing there in their white coats, or long black cassocks, staring down the passage.

A great hush hung over everything, and through the hush we slid into the awful streets again, with the houses lying on the ground.

Before we had gone far, we heard shouts, and turning my head I discovered some wounded soldiers, limping along a side-road, who were begging us to give them a lift towards the boat.

We filled the car so full that we all had to stand up, except those who could not stand.

Bandaged heads and faces were all around me, while bandaged soldiers rode on the foot-board, clinging to whatever they could get hold of, and then we moved towards the quay. It was heartbreaking to have to deny the scores of limping, broken men who shouted to us to stop, but as soon as we had deposited one load we went back and picked up others and ran them back to the quay, and that we did time after time. A few of the men were our own Tommies, but most were Belgians. Backwards and forwards we rushed, backwards and forwards, and now that dear Henri's eyes were shining, his sallow, pie-coloured face was lit up, he no longer looked tired and dull and heavy, he was on fire with excitement. And the car raced like mad backwards and forwards, backwards and forwards, venturing right out towards the forts and back again to the quay, until at last reaction set in with Henri and he was obliged to take the car back to the hotel, where he fell in a crumpled heap in a corner of the restaurant.

As we came in the patronne handed me a note.

"While you were out,"she said, looking at me sorrowfully, "M. Fox and M. Jones returned on their bicycles to look for you."

Then I read Mr. Fox's kind message.

"We have managed to secure passages on a special military boat for

Flushing that leaves at half-past eleven and of course we have got one for you. We have come back for you, but you are not here. Your car has arrived, so you will be all right, I hope. You have seen the bombardment through, bravo!"

I was glad they had got away. But for myself some absolutely irresistible force held me to Antwerp, and I now slipped quietly out of the hotel and started off on a solitary walk.

CHAPTER XXXVI

A SOLITARY WALK

Surely, surely, this livid, copper-tinted noontide, hanging over Antwerp, was conceived in Hades as a presentation of the world's last day.

Indescribably terrible in tone and form, because of its unearthly qualities of smoke, shrapnel, petroleum-fumes, and broken, dissipated clouds, the darkened skies seemed of themselves to offer every element of tragedy, while the city lying stretched out beneath in that agony of silence, that lasted from twelve o'clock to half-past one, was one vast study in blood, fire, ruined houses, ruined pathways, smoke, appalling odours, heartbreak and surrender. The last steamer had gone from the Port. The last of the fleeing inhabitants had departed by the Breda Gate. All that was left now was the empty city, waiting for the entrance of the Germans.

Empty were the streets. Empty were the boats, crowded desolately on the Scheldt. Empty were those hundreds of deserted motor cars, heaped in great weird, pathetic piles down at the water's edge, as useless as though they were perambulators, because there were no chauffeurs to drive them. Empty was the air of sound except for the howling of dogs that ran about in terror, crying miserably for their owners who had been obliged to desert them. Through the emptiness of the air, when the dogs were not howling, resounded only a terrible, ferocious silence, that seemed to call up mocking memories of the noise the shells had been making incessantly, ever since two nights ago.

It was an hour never to be forgotten, an hour that could never, never come again.

I kept saying that to myself as I continued my solitary walk.

"Solitary walk!"

For the first time in a lifetime that bit of journalese took on a meaning so deep and elemental, that it went right down to the very roots of the language. The whole city was mine. I seemed to be the only living being left. I passed hundreds of tall, white, stately houses, all shattered and locked and silent and deserted. I went through one wide, deadly street after another. I looked up and down the great paralysed quays. I stared through the yellow avenues of trees. I heard my own footsteps echoing, echoing. The ghosts of five hundred thousand people floated before my vision. For weeks, for months, I had seen these five hundred thousand people laughing and talking in these very streets. And yesterday, and the day before, I had seen them fleeing for their lives out of the city – anywhere, anywhere, out of the reach of the shells and the Germans.

And I wondered where they were now, those five hundred thousand ghosts.

Were they still struggling and tramping and falling along the roads to Holland?

As I wondered, I kept on seeing their faces in these their doorways and at these their windows. I saw them seated at these their cafes, along the side-paths. I heard their rich, liquid Antwerp voices speaking French with a soft, swift rush, or twanging away at Flemish with the staccato insistence of Flanders. I felt them all around me, in all the deserted streets, at all the shuttered windows. It was too colossal a thing to realise that the five hundred thousand of them were not in their city any longer, that they were not hiding behind the silence and the shutters, but were out in the open world beyond the city gates, fighting their way to Holland and freedom.

And now I wondered why I was here myself, listening to my echoing footsteps through the hollow silences of the "Ville Morte."

Why had I not gone with the rest of them?

Then, as I walked through the dead city I knew why I was there.

It was because the gods had been keeping for me all these years the supreme gift of this solitary walk, when I should share her death-pangs with this city I so passionately loved.

That was the truth. I had been unable to tear myself away. If Antwerp suffered, I desired to suffer too. I desired to go hand in hand with her in whatever happened when the Germans came marching in.

Many a time before had I loved a city – loved her for her beauty, her fairness, her spirit, her history, her personal significance to me. Pietra Santa, Ravenna, Bibbiena, Poppi, Locarno, Verona, Florence, Venice, Rome, Sydney, Colombo, Aries, London, Parma, for one reason or another I have worshipped you all in your turn! One represents beauty, one work, one love, one sadness, one joy, one the escape from the ego, one the winging of ambition, one sheer sestheticism, one liquid, limpid gladness at discovering oneself alive.

But Antwerp was the first and only city that I loved because she let me share her sufferings with her right through the Valley of Death, right up to the moment when she breathed her last sigh as a city, and passed into the possession of her conquerors.

Suddenly, through the terrific, inconceivable lull, hurtling with a million memories of noises, I heard footsteps, heavy, dragging, yet hurried, and looking up a side-street opposite the burning ruins of the Chaussée de Souliers, I saw two Belgian soldiers, limping along, making towards the Breda Gate.

Both were wounded, and the one who was less bad was helping the other.

They were hollow-cheeked, hollow-eyed, starved, ghastly, with a growth of black beard, and the ravages of smoke and powder all over their poor faded blue uniforms and little scarlet and yellow caps.

They were dazed, worn-out, finished, famished, nearly fainting.

But as they hurried past me the younger man flung out one breathless question:

"*Est-ce que la ville est prise?*"

It seemed to be plucked from some page of Homer.

Its potency was so epic, so immense, that I felt as if I must remain there for ever rooted to the spot where I had heard it...

It went thrilling through my being. It struck me harder than any shell, seeming to fell me for a moment to the ground...

Then I rose, permeated with a sense of living in the world's greatest drama, and *feeling*, not *seeing*, Art and Life and Death and Literature inextricably and terribly, yet gloriously mixed, till one could not be told from the other...

For he who had given his life, whose blood dropped red from him as he moved, knew not what had happened to his city.

He was only a soldier!

His was to fight, not to know.

"Est-ce que la ville est prise?"

It is months since then, but I still hear that perishing soldier's voice, breaking over his terrific query.

* * * *

...Presently, rousing myself, I ran onwards and walked beside the men, giving my arm to the younger one, who took it mechanically, without thanking me.

I liked that, and all together we hastened through the livid greyness along the Avenue de Commerce, towards the Breda Gate.

In dead silence we laboured onwards.

It was still a solitary walk, for neither of my companions said a word.

Only sometimes, without speaking, one of them would turn his head and look backwards, without stopping, at the red flames reflected in the black sky to northward.

Suddenly, to our amazement, we saw a cart coming down a side-street, containing a man and a little girl.

I ran like lightning towards it, terrified lest it should pass, but that man in the cart had a soul, he had seen the bleeding soldiers, he was stopping of himself, he offered to take me, too.

"Quick, quick, mes amis!" he said. "The Germans are coming in at the other end even now! The petite here was lost, and thanks to the Bon Dieu I have just found her. That is why I am so late."

As the soldiers crawled painfully into the little cart, I whispered to the elder one:

"Do you know where your King is, Monsieur?"

Ah, the flash in that hollow eye!

It was worth risking one's life to see it, and to hear the love that leapt into the Belgian's voice as he answered:

"Truly, I know not exactly! But wherever he is I *do* know this. *Notre Roi est sur le Champ de Bataille*"

Oh, beautiful speech!

"Sur le Champ de Bataille!"

Where else would Albert be indeed?

"Sur le Champ de Bataille!"

I put it beside the Epic Question!

Together they lie there in my heart, imperishable, and more precious than any written poem!

CHAPTER XXXVII

ENTER LES ALLEMANDS

It is now half-past one, and I am back at the hotel.

At least, my watch says it is half-past one.

But all the many great gold-faced clocks in Antwerp have stopped the day before, and their hands point mockingly to a dozen different times.

One knows that only some ghastly happening could have terrified them into such wild mistakes.

Heart-breaking it is, as well as appalling, to see those distracted timepieces, and their ignorance of the fatal hour.

Half-past one!

And the clocks point pathetically to eleven, or eight, or five.

Inside the great dim restaurant a pretence of lunch is going on between the little handful of people left.

Everybody sits at one table, the chauffeur, Henri, the refugees from Lierre, their maidservant, Jeannette, the proprietor, and his old sister, and his two little grandchildren, and their father, the porter, and a couple of very ugly old Belgians, who seem to belong to nobody in particular, and have sprung from nobody knows where.

We have some stewed meat with potatoes, a rough, ill-cooked dish.

This is the first bad meal I have had in Antwerp.

But what seems extraordinary to me, is that there should be any meal at all!

As we sit round the table in the darkness of that lurid noontide, the dead city outside looks in through the broken windows, and there comes over us all a tension so great that nobody can utter a word.

We are all thinking the same thing.

We are thinking with our dull, adled, clouded brains that the Germans will be here at any minute.

And then suddenly the waiter cries out in a loud voice from across the restaurant:

"LES ALLEMANDS!"

We all spring to our feet. We stand for a moment petrified.

Through the great uncurtained windows of the hotel we see one grey figure, and then another, walking along the side-path up the Avenue de Commerce.

"They have come!" says everyone.

After a moment's hesitation M. Claude, the proprietor, and his old sister, move out into the street, and mechanically I, and all the others follow as if afraid to be left alone within.

CHAPTER XXXVIII

"MY SON!"

And now through the livid sunless silences of the deserted city, still reeking horribly of powder, shrapnel, smoke and burning petroleum, the Germans are coming down the Avenues to enter into possession.

Here they come, a long grey line of foot-soldiers and mounted men, all with pink roses or carnations in their grey tunics.

Suddenly, a long, lidded, baker's cart dashes across the road at a desperate rate, wheeled by a poor old Belgian, whose face is so wild, that I whisper as she passes close to me:

"Is somebody ill in your cart?"

Without stopping, without looking even, her haggard eyes full of despair, she mutters:

"*Dead!* My son! He was a soldat."

Then she hurries on, at a run now, to find a spot where she can hide or bury her beloved before the Germans are all over the city.

CHAPTER XXXIX

THE RECEPTION

A singular change now comes over the silent, deserted city.

First, a few stray Belgians shew on the side-paths. Then more appear, and more still, and as the procession of the Germans comes onwards through the town I discover little groups of men and women sprung out of the very earth it seems to me.

All along the Avenue de Commerce, gathered in the heavy greyness on the side-paths, are little straggling groups of *Anversois*.

As I look at them, I suddenly experience a sensation of suffocation. Am I dreaming?

Or are they really *smiling*, those people, *smiling to the Germans!*

Then, to my horror, I see two old men waving gaily to that long grey oncoming line of men and horses.

And then I see a woman flinging flowers to an officer, who catches them and sticks them into his horse's bridle.

At that moment I realise I am in for some extraordinary experience, something that Brussels has not in the least prepared me for!

CHAPTER XL

THE LAUGHTER OF BRUTES

Along the Avenue the grey uniforms are slowly marching, headed by fair, blue-eyed, arrogant officers on splendid roan horses, and the clang and clatter of them breaks up the silence with a dramatic sharpness – the silence that has never been heard in Antwerp since!

As they come onward, the Germans look from left to right.

I stand on the pavement watching, drawn there by some irresistible force.

Eagerly I search their faces, looking now for the horrid marks of the brute triumphant, gloating over his prey. But the brute triumphant is not there to-day, for these thousands of Germans who march into Antwerp on this historic Friday, are characterised by an aspect of dazed incredulity that almost amounts to fear.

They all wear pink roses, or carnations, in their coats, or have pink flowers wreathed about their horses' harness or round their gun-carriages and provision motors; and sometimes they burst into subdued singing; but it is obvious that the enormous buildings of Antwerp, and its aspect of great wealth, and solidarity, fairly take away their breath, and their eyes quite plainly say that they cannot understand how they come to be in possession of this great, rich, wonderful prize.

They look to left and right, their blue eyes full of curiosity. As I watch, I think of Bismarck's remark about London: *What a city to loot!*

That same thought is in the eyes of all these thousands of Germans as they come in to take possession of Antwerp, and they suddenly burst into song, "Pappachen," and "Die Wacht am Rhein."

But never very cheerily or very loudly do they sing.

I fancy at that moment, experiencing as they are that phase of naive and genuine amazement, the Germans are really less brute than usual.

And then, just as I am thinking that, I meet with my first personal experience of the meaning of. *"German brute."*

A young officer has espied a notice-board, high above a cafe on the left.

A delighted grin overspreads his face and he quickly draws his companion's attention to it.

Together the two gaze smiling at the homelike words: *"WINTER GARTEN,"* their blue eyes glued upon the board as they ride along.

The contrast between their gladness, and that old Belgian mother's agony, suddenly strikes through my heart like a knife.

The pathos and tragedy of it all are too much for me. To see this beloved city possessed by Germans is too terrible. Yes, standing there in the beautiful Avenue de Commerce, I weep as if it were London itself that the Germans were coming into, for I have lived for long unforgettable weeks among the Belgians at war, and I have learned to love and respect them above all peoples. And so I stand there in the Avenue with tears rolling down my cheeks, watching the passing of the grey uniforms, with my heart all on fire for poor ruined Belgium.

Then, looking up, I see a young Prussian officer laughing at me mockingly as he rides by.

He laughs and looks away, that smart young grey-clad Uhlan, with roses in his coat; then he looks back, and laughs again, and rides on, still laughing mockingly at what he takes to be some poor little Belgian weeping over the destruction of her city.

To me, that is an act of brutality, that, small as it may seem, counts for a barbarity as great as any murder.

Germany, for that brutal laugh, no less than for your outrages, you shall pay some day, you shall surely pay!

CHAPTER XLI

TRAITORS

And now I see people gathering round the Germans as they come to a halt at the end of the Avenue. I see people stroking the horses' heads, and old men and young men smiling and bowing, and a few minutes later, inside the restaurant of my hotel, I witness those extraordinary encounters between the Germans and their spies. I hear the clink of gold, and see the passing of big German notes, and I watch the flushed faces of Antwerp men who are holding note-books over the tables to the German officers, and drinking beer with them, to the accompaniment of loud riotous laughter. That is the note struck in the first hour of the German entrance; and that is the note all the time as far as the German-Anversois are concerned. Before very long I discover that there must have been hundreds of people hiding away inside those silent houses, waiting for the Germans to come in. The horror of it makes me feel physically ill.

The procession comes to a standstill at last in front of a little green square by the Athene, and next moment a group of grey-clad officers with roses in their tunics are hurrying towards the hotel, and begin parleying with Monsieur Claude, our proprietor.

I expected to see him icily resolute against receiving them. But to my surprise he seems affable. He smiles. He waves his hand as he talks. He is eager, deferential, and quite unmistakably friendly, friendly even to the point of fawning. Turning, he flings open his doors with a bow, and in a few minutes the Germans are crowding into his great restaurants.

Cries of "Bier" resounded on all sides.

Outside, on the walls of the Theatre Flamand, the Huns are at it already with their endless proclamations.

EINWOHNER VON ANTWERPEN!

Das deutsche Heer betritt Euere Stadt als Sieger. Keinem Euerer Mitbürger wird ein Leid geschehen und, Euer Eigentum wird geschont werden, wenn ihr Euch jeder Feindseligkeit enthaltet.

Jede Widersetzlichkeit dagegen wird nach Kriegsrecht bestraft und kann die Zerstörung Euerer schönen Stadt zur Folge haben.

DER OBERBEFEHLSHABER DER
DEUTSCHEN TRUPPEN.

INWONERS VAN ANTWERPEN!

Het Duitsche leger is als overwinnaar in uwe stad gekomen. Aan geen enkel uwer medeburgers zal eenig leed geschieden en uwe eigendommen zullen ongeschonden blijven, wanneer gij u allenvan vijandelijkheden onthoudt.

Elk verzet zal naar oorlogsrecht worden bestraft en kan de vernietiging van uwe schoone stad voor gevolg hebben.

DE HOOFDBEVELHEBBER DER
DUITSCHE TROEPEN.

HABITANTS D'AN VERS!

L'armèe allemande est entree dans votre ville en vainquer. Aucun de vos concitoyens ne sera inquiété et vos propriétés seront respectées a la condition que vous vous absteniez de toute hostilite.

Toute resistance sera punie d'apres les lois de la guerre, et peut entrainer la destruction de votre belle ville.

LE COMMANDANT EN CHEF DES
TROUPES CHEF ALLEMANDS.

CHAPTER XLII

WHAT THE WAITING MAID SAW

At this point, I crept down steathily into the kitchen and proceeded to disguise myself.

I put on first of all a big blue-and-red check apron. Then I pinned a black shawl over my shoulders. I parted my hair in the middle and twisted it into a little tight knot at the back, and I tied a blue-and-white handkerchief under my chin.

Looking thoroughly hideous I slipped back into the restaurant where I occupied myself with washing and drying glasses behind the counter.

It was a splendid point of observation, and no words can tell of the excitement I felt as I stooped over my work and took in every detail of what was going on in the restaurant.

But sometimes the glasses nearly fell from my fingers, so agonising were the sights I saw in that restaurant at Antwerp, on the afternoon of October 9th – the Fatal Friday.

I saw old men and young men crowding round the Germans. They sat at the tables with them drinking, laughing, and showing their note-books, which the Germans eagerly examined. The air resound-ed with their loud riotous talk. All shame was thrown aside now. For months these spies must have lived in terror as they carried on their nefarious espionage within the walls of Antwerp. But now their ter-ror was over. The Germans were in possession. They had nothing to fear. So they drank deeply and more deeply still, trying to banish from their eyes that furtive look that marked them for the sneaks they

were. Some of them were old greybeards, some of them were chic
young men. I recognised several of them as people I had seen about
in the streets of Antwerp during those past two months, and again
and again burning tears gathered in my eyes as I realised how
Antwerp had been betrayed.

As I am turning this terrible truth over in my mind I get another
violent shock. I see three Englishmen standing in the middle of the
now densely-crowded restaurant. At first I imagine they are prisoners, and a wave of sorrow flows over me. For I know those three men;
they are the three English Marines who called in at this hotel yesterday; seeing that they were Englishmen by their uniforms I called to
them to keep back a savage dog that was trying to get at the cocka-
too that I had rescued from Lierre. They told me they were with the
rest of the English Flying Corps at the forts. Their English had been
perfect. Never for a minute had I suspected them!

And now, here they are still, in their English uniforms, and little
black-peaked English caps, talking German with the Germans, and
sitting at a little table, drinking, drinking, and laughing boisterously
as only Germans can laugh when they hold their spying councils.

English Marines indeed!

They have stolen our uniforms somehow, and have probably
betrayed many a secret. Within the next few hours I am forced to the
conclusion that Antwerp is one great nest of German spies, and over
and over again I recognised the faces of old men and young men
whom I have seen passing as honest Antwerp citizens all these
months.

Seated all by himself at a little table sits a Belgian General, who has
been brought in prisoner.

In his sadness and dignity he makes an unforgettable picture. His
black beard is sunk forward on his chest. His eyes are lowered. His
whole being seem to be wrapt in a profound melancholy that yet has
something magnificent and distinguished about it when compared
with the riotous elation of his conquerors.

Nobody speaks to him. He speaks to nobody. With his dark blue cloak flung proudly across his shoulder he remains mute and motionless as a statue, his dark eyes staring into space. I wonder what his thoughts are as he sees before him, unashamed and unafraid now that German occupation has begun, these spies who have bartered their country for gold. But whatever he thinks, that lonely prisoner, he makes no sign. His dignity is inviolable. His dark bearded face has all the poignancy and beauty of Titian's "Ariosto" in the National Gallery in London.

He is a prisoner. Nobody looks at him. Nobody speaks to him. Nobody gives him anything to eat. Exhaustion is written on his face. At last I can bear it no longer. I pour out a cup of hot coffee, and take a sandwich from the counter. Then I slip across the Restaurant, and put the coffee and the sandwich on the little table in front of him. A look of flashing gratitude and surprise is in his dark sad eyes as they lift themselves for a moment. But I dare not linger. The Flemish maid, with the handkerchief across her head, hurries back to her tumblers.

Two little priests have been brought in as prisoners also.

But they chat cheerily with their captors, who look down upon them smilingly, showing their big white teeth in a way that I would not like if I were a prisoner!

None of the prisoners are handcuffed or surrounded. They do not seem to be watched. They are all left free. So free indeed, that it is difficult to realise the truth – one movement towards the door and they would be shot down like dogs!

In occupying a town without resistance the Germans make themselves as charming as possible. Obviously those are their orders from headquarters. And Germans always obey orders. Extraordinary indeed is the discipline that can turn the brutes of Louvain and Aerschot into the lamb-like beings that took possession of Antwerp. They asked for everything with marked courtesy, even gentleness. They paid for everything they got. I heard some of the poorer soldiers expressing their surprise at the price of the Antwerp beer.

"It's too dear!" they said.

But they paid the price for it all the same.

They always waited patiently until they could be served. They never grumbled. They never tried to rush the people who were serving them. In fact, their system was to give no trouble, and to create as good an impression as possible on the Belgians from the first moment of their entrance – the first moment being by far the most important psychologically, as the terrified brains of the populace are then most receptive to their impressions of the hated army, and anything that could be done to enhance and improve those impressions is more valuable then than at any other time.

Almost the first thing the Germans did was to find out the pianos.

It was not half an hour after they entered Antwerp when strains of music were heard, music that fell on the ear with a curious shock, for no one had played the piano here since the Belgian Government moved into the fortified town. They played beautifully, those Germans, and every now and then they burst into song. From the sitting-rooms in the Hotel I heard them singing to the "Blue Danube." And the "Wacht am Rhein" seemed to come and go at intervals, like a leitmotif to all their doings.

About four o'clock, Jeanette, the Flemish servant, whispered to me that Henri wanted to speak to me in the kitchen.

"A great misfortune has happened, Madame!" said Henri, agitatedly. "The Germans have seized my car. I shall not be able to take you out of Antwerp this afternoon. But courage! to-morrow I will find a cart or a fiacre. To-day it is impossible to do anything, there is not a vehicle of any kind to be had. But to-morrow, Madame, trust Henri f He will get you away, never fear!"

Half an hour after, the faithful fellow called to me again.

His pie-coloured face looked dark and miserable.

"The Germans have shut the gates all round the city and no one is allowed to go in and out without a German passport!" he said.

This was serious.

Relying on my experience in Brussels, I had anticipated being able to get away even more easily from Antwerp, because of Henri's motor car. But obviously for the moment I was checked.

As dusk fell and the lights were lit, I retired into the kitchen and busied myself cutting bread and butter, and still continuing my highly interesting observations. On the table lay piles of sausage, and presently in came two German officers, an old grey-bearded General, and a dashing young Uhlan Lieutenant.

"We want three eggs each," said the Uhlan roughly, addressing himself to me. "Three eggs, soft boiled, and some bread with butter, with much butter!"

I nodded but dared not answer.

And the red-faced young Lieutenant, thinking I did not understand, ground his heel angrily, and muttered "Gott!" when his eyes fell on the sausage, and his expression changed as if by magic.

"Wurst?" he ejaculated to the General. "Here there sausage is!"

It was quite funny to see the way these two gallant soldiers bent over the sausage, their eyes beaming with greedy joy, and in ten minutes every German was crying out for sausage, and the town was being ransacked in all directions in search of more.

CHAPTER XLIII

SATURDAY

The saddest thing in Antwerp is the howling of the dogs.

Thousands have been left shut in the houses when their owners fled, and all day and night these poor creatures utter piercing, desolate cries that grow louder and more piercing as time goes on.

It is Saturday morning, October 10th.

Strange things have happened.

When I went to my door just now, I found it locked from the outside.

I have tried the other door. That is locked, too.

What does it mean, I wonder?

Here I am in a little room about twelve feet by six, with one window looking on to the back wall of one of the Antwerp theatres.

I can hear the sounds of fierce cannonading going on in the distance, but the noise within the hotel close at hand is so loud as to deaden the sounds of battle; for the Germans are running up and down the corridors perpetually, shouting, singing, stamping, and the pianos are going, too.

Nobody comes near me. I knock at both the doors, but gently, for I am afraid to draw attention to myself. Nobody answers. The old woman and the two little children have left the room on my right, the old man has left the room on my left. I am all alone in this little den. I dress as well as I can, but the room is just a tiny sitting-room; there are no facilities for making one's toilette. I have to do without washing my face. Instead, I rub it with Creme Floreine, and the amount of black that comes off is appalling.

Then I lie down at full length on my mattress and wonder what is going to happen next.

Hour after hour goes by.

In a corner of the room I discover an English weekly history of the War, and lying there on my mattress I read many strange stories that seem somehow to mock a little at these real happenings.

Then voices just outside in the corridor reach me.

Out there two old Belgians are talking.

"*Ce sont les Anglais qui ne veulent pas rendre les forts!*" says one.

They are discussing the fighting which still goes on fiercely in the forts around the city.

My head aches! I am hungry; and those big guns are making what the Kaiser would call World Noises.

Strange thoughts come over me, attacking me, like Samson Agonistes' "deadly swarm of hornets armed." [9]

In a terrific conflict it doesn't seem to matter much which side is victorious, all hatred of the conquerors dies away; in fact the conquerors themselves may seem like deliverers since peace comes in with their entrance.

And I am weak and weary enough at this moment to wish *les Anglais* would give it up, let the forts be rendered, and let the cannons cease.

Anything for peace, for an end of slaughter, an end of terror, an end of this cruel soul-racking thunder.

Terrible thoughts... deadly thoughts.

Do they come to the soldiers, thoughts like these? Heaven help the poor fellows if they do!

They are more deadly than Death, for they attack only the immortal part of one, leaving the mortal to save itself while they blight and corrode the spirit.

[9] Verses 19-20 from *Samson Agoniste* by John Milton, first published in 1671.

* * * *

I am weary. I have not slept for five nights, and I feel as if I shall never sleep again.

I daresay that's partly why I have been weak enough to wish for an end of noise.

It's five o'clock and darkness has set in.

Nobody has been near me, I'm still here, locked up in this little room.

I roam about like a caged animal. I look from the window. The blank back wall of the Antwerp Theatre meets my eye, but a corner of the hotel looks in also, and I can see three tiers of windows, so I hastily move away. In all those rooms there are Germans quartered now. What if they glanced down here and discovered *me*? I pull the curtains over the window, and move back into the room.

This is Saturday afternoon, October 10th, and all of a sudden a queer thought comes over me.

October 10th is my birthday.

I lie down on the mattress again, and my thoughts begin dreamily to revolve round an extraordinary psychic mystery that I became conscious of when I was little more than a baby in far-away Australia.

I became conscious at the age of four that I heard in my imagination the sounds of cannon, and I became certain too that those cannon were going to be real cannon some day.

Yes! All my life, ever since I could think, I have heard heavy firing in my ears, and have known I was going to be very close to battle, some far-off day or other.

Have other people been born with the same belief, I wonder?

I should like so much to know.

Gradually a vast area of speculative psychology opens out before me, and, like one walking in a world of dreams, I lose myself in its dim distances, seeking for some light, clear opening, wherein I can discover the secret of this extraordinary psychic or physiological mystery, that has hidden itself for a lifetime in my being. I say hidden itself; yet, though it has kept itself dark and concealed, it has always been teasing my sub-consciousness with vague queer hints of its presence, until at last I have grown used to if, and have even arranged a fairly comfortable explanation of its existence between my soul and myself.

I have told myself that it is something I can never, never understand. And that it is all the explanation I have ever been able to give to myself of the presence of this uninvited guest who has dwelt for a lifetime in the secret-chambers of my intuitions, who has hidden there, veiled and mysterious, never shewing a simple feature to betray itself – eye, lips, brow – always remaining unseen, unknown, uninvited, unintelligible – yet always potent, always softly disturbing one's belief in one's ordinary everyday life with that dull roar of cannon which seemed to visualize in my brain with an image of blinding sunlight.

Lying there on the bare mattress, on this drear October day which goes down to history as the day on which Germany set up her Governor in Antwerp, I begin to wonder if my sublimable consciousness has been trying, all these years, to warn me that danger would come to me some day to the sound of battle. And am I in that danger now? Is this the moment perhaps that the secret, silent guest has tried to shew me lay lurking in await for me, ready to make me fulfil my destiny in some dark and terrible way?

No. I can't believe it.

I can't see it like that.

I *don't* believe that that is what the roar of cannon has been trying to say to me all my life.

I can't sense danger – I won't. No, I mean I *can't*. My reason assures me there isn't any danger that is going to *catch* me, no matter how it may threaten.

And then the hornet flies to the attack.

"It says, 'People who are haunted with premonitions nearly always disregard them until too late.' "

So occupied am I with these dreams and philosophings that I lie there in the darkness, forgetful of time and hunger, until I hear voices in the next room, and there is the old woman opening my door, and the two little yellow-haired children staring in at me curiously.

The old woman gives me some grapes out of a basket under her bed, and a glass of water.

"*Pauvre enfant!*" she says. "I am sorry I could bring you no food, but the Germans are up and down the stairs all day long, and I dare not risk them asking me, "Who is that for?"

"But why are you so afraid?"I ask." Last night you were so nice to me. What has happened? Come, tell me the truth."

"Alors, Madame, I will tell you! You recollect that German who leaned over the counter for such a long time when you were washing glasses?"

"Yes." My lips felt suddenly dry as wood.

"Alors, Madame! He said to me, that fellow, ' *She* never speaks!' "

"Who did he mean?"

"Alors, Madame, he meant you!"

(This then, I think to myself, is what happens to one when one is really frightened. The lips turn dry as chips. And all because a German has noticed me. It is absurd.)

I force a smile.

"Perhaps you imagine this," I said.

"No, because he said to me to-day, 'Where is that mädchen who never spoke?' "

"What did you say?"

"She is deaf," I told him. "She does not hear when anyone speaks to her!"

"So that is why you locked me up."

"*Cest ca*, Madame. It was my brother who wished it. He is very afraid. And now, Madame, good-night. I must put the little girls to bed."

"Well, I think this is ridiculous," I said. "How long am I to stay here?"

She shook her head, and began to unfasten little fair-haired Maria's black serge frock, pushing her out of my room as she did so, with the evident intention of locking me in again.

But just then someone knocked at the outer door.

It was Madame X. who came stealing in, drawing the bolt noiselessly behind her. I looked in her weary face, with its white hair, and beautiful blue eyes, and saw gentleness and sympathy there, and sincerity.

She said: "Mon Mari has been talking in the restaurant with a friend of his, a Danish Doctor, a Red Cross Doctor, Madame, you understand, and oh, he is so sorry for you, Madame, and he thinks he can help you to escape! He wants to come up and see you for a moment. I advise you to see him."

"Will you bring him up," I said.

"Immediately!"

The old patronne went on undressing the little girls, getting them hurriedly into bed and telling them to be quiet.

They kept shouting out questions to me, and whenever they did so their grandmother would smack them.

"Silence. *Les alboches* will hear you!"

But they were terribly naughty little girls.

Whenever I spoke they repeated my words in loud, mocking voices.

Their sharp little ears told them of my foreign accent, and they plucked at every strange note in my voice, and repeated it loud and shrill, but the grandmother smacked them into silence and pulled the bedclothes up over their faces.

Then a gentle tap, and Madame X. and the Danish Doctor came stealing in.

Ah! how piercing and pathetic was the look I cast on that tall stranger. I saw a young fair-haired man in grey clothes, with blue eyes, and an honest English look, quiet, kind, sincere, wearing the Red Gross badge on his arm! I looked and looked. Then I told myself he was to be trusted.

In English he said, "I heard there was an English lady here who wants to get away from Antwerp?"

I interrupted sharply.

"Please don't speak English! The Germans are always going up and down the corridor. They may hear!"

He smiled at my fears, but immediately changed into French to reassure me.

"No, no, Madame! You mustn't be alarmed. The Germans are too busy with themselves to think of anything else just now. And I want to help you. Your Queen Alexandra is a Dane. She is of my country, and she has kept the bonds very close and strong between Denmark and England. Yes, if only for the sake of Queen Alexandra I want to help you now. And I think I can do so. If you will pass as my sister I can get a pass for you from the Danish Consul, and that will enable you to leave Antwerp in safety."

"May I see your papers?" I asked him now. "I am sure you are sincere. But you understand that I would like to see your papers."

"Certainly!"

And he brought out his papers of nationality and I saw that he was undoubtedly a Dane, working under the Red Cross for the Belgians.

When I had examined his papers I let him examine mine.

"And now I must ask you one thing more," he said. "I must ask for your passport. I want to shew it to my Consul, in order to convince him that you are really of British nationality. Will you give me your passport? I am afraid that without it my Consul may object to do this thing for me."

That was an agonized moment. I had been told a hundred times by a hundred different people that the one thing one should never do, never, never, never, not under any circumstances, was to part with one's passport. And here was this gentle Dane pleading for mine, promising me escape if I would give it. I looked up at him as he stood there, tall and grave. I was not *quite* sure of him. And why? Because he had spoken English and I still thought that was a dangerous thing to do. No, I was not quite sure. I stood there breathless, stupefied, trying to think. Madame X. watched me in silence. I knew that I must make up my mind one way or the other.

"Well, I shall trust you," I said slowly. I put my passport into his hands.

His face lit up and I, watching in that agony of doubt, told myself suddenly that he was genuine, that was real gladness in his eyes.

"Ah, Madame, I *do* thank you so for trusting me!" His voice was moved and vibrant. He bent and kissed my hand. Then he put the passport in his pocket." To-morrow at three o'clock I will come here for you. Trust me absolutely. I will arrange for a peasant's cart or a fiacre, and I will myself accompany you to the Dutch borders. Have courage – you will soon be in safety!"

Ten minutes after he had gone Monsieur Claude burst into the room.

His face was black as night and working with rage.

"What is this you have done?" he cried in a hoarse voice. *"Il parle avec les allemands dans le restaurant!"*

Horrible words!

It seems to me that as long as I live I shall hear them in my ears.

"It is not true." I cried. "It *can't* be true."

"He is talking to the Germans in the Restaurant," he repeated. His rage was undisguised. He flung on the table a little packet of English papers that I had given him to hide for me. "Take these! I have nothing to do with you. You are my sister's affair, I have nothing to do with you at all!"

I rushed to him. I seized him by the arm. But he flung me off and left the room. In and out of my brain his words went beating, in and out, in and out. The thing was simple, clear. The Dane had gone down to betray me, and he had all the evidence in his hands. Oh, fool that I had been! I had brought this on myself. It was my own unaccountable folly that had led me into this trap. At any moment now the Germans would come for me. All was over. I was lost. They had my passport in their possession. I could deny nothing.   The game was up.

I got up and looked at myself in the glass.

The habit of a lifetime asserted itself, for all women look at themselves in the glass frequently, and at unexpected times. I saw a strange white face gazing at me in the mirror. "It is all up with you now! Are you ready for the end? Prepare yourself, get your nerves in order. You cannot hope to escape, it is either imprisonment or death for you! What do you think of that?"

And then, at that point, kindly Mother Nature took possession of the situation and sleep rushed upon me unawares. I fell on the mattress and knew no more, till a soft knocking at my door awoke me, and I saw it was morning. A light was filtering in dimly through the window blind.

I jumped up.

I was fully dressed, having fallen asleep in my clothes.

"Madame!" whispered a voice. "Open the door toute suite n'est-ce-pas." It was the old woman's voice.

I pulled away the barricading chair, and let her in.

Over her shoulder I saw a man.

It was no German, this!

It was dear pie-coloured Henri in a grey suit with a white-and-black handkerchief swathed round his neck.

Behind him were the two little girls.

"Quick, quick!" breathes the old woman, "you must go, Madame, you must go at once! My brother is frightened; he refuses to have you here any longer. He is terrified out of his life lest the Germans should discover that he has been allowing an English woman to hide in his house!"

She threw an apron on me, and hurriedly tied it behind me, then she brought out a big black shawl and flung it round my shoulders. Then she picked up the blue-and-white check handkerchief lying on the table, and nodded to me to tie it over my head.

"You must go at once, you must leave everything behind you. You must not take anything. We will see about your things afterwards. You must pass as Henri's wife. There! Take his arm! And you, Henri, take one of the little girls by the hand! And you, Madame, you take the other. There! Courage, Madame. Oh, my poor child, I am sorry for you!"

She kissed me, and pushed me out at the same time.

Next moment, hanging on to Henri's arm, I found myself outside in the corridor walking towards the staircase.

"Courage!" whispered Henri in my ear.

Suddenly I ceased to be myself; I became a peasant; I was Henri's wife. These little girls were mine. I leaned on Henri, I clutched my little girl's fingers close. I felt utterly unafraid. I thought as a peasant. I absolutely precipitated myself into the woman I was supposed to be. And in that new condition of personality I walked down the wide staircase with my husband and my children, passing dozens of German officers who were running up and down the stairs continually.

I got a touch of their system. They moved aside to let us pass, the poor little pie-coloured peasant, his anxious wife, the two solemn children with flowing hair.

The hall below was crowded with Germans. I saw their fair florid faces, their grim lips and blazing eyes. But I was a peasant now, a little Belgian peasant. Reality had left me completely. Fear was fled. The sight of the sunlight and the touch of the fresh air on my face as we reached the street set all my nerves acting again in their old satisfactory manner.

"Courage, Madame!" whispered Henri.

"Don't call me Madame! Call me Louisa!" I whispered back. "Where are we going?"

"To a friend."

We turned the corner and crossed the street and I saw at once that Antwerp as Antwerp has entirely ceased to exist. Everywhere there were Germans. They were seated in the cafes, flying past in motor cars, driving through the streets and avenues just as in Brussels, looking as if they had lived there for ever.

"Voici, Madame!" muttered Henri.

"Louisa!" I whispered supplicatingly.

CHAPTER XLIV

CAN I TRUST THEM?

We entered a cafe. I shrank and clutched his arm. The place was full of Germans, but they were common soldiers these, not Officers. They were drinking beer and coffee at the little tables.

"Take no notice of them!" whispered Henri. "You are all right! Trust me!"

We walked through the Restaurant, Henri and I arm in arm, and the little girls clinging to our hands.

They really played their parts amazingly, those little girls.

"I have found my wife from Brussels," announced Henri in a loud voice to the old proprietor behind the counter.

"How are things in Brussels, Madame?" queried an old Belgian in the cafe.

But I made no answer.

I affected not to hear.

I went with Henri on through the little hall at the far end of the cafe.

Next moment I found myself in a big, clean kitchen. And a tall stout woman, her black eyes swimming in tears, was leaning towards me, her arms open.

"Oh, poor Madame!" she said.

She clasped me to her breast.

Between her tears, in her choking voice she whispered, "I told Henri to bring you here. You are safe with me. We are from Luxemburg. We fled from home at the beginning of the war rather than see our state swarming with Prussians, as it is now. We Luxemburgers hate Germans with a hate that passes all other hate on earth. And I have three children, who are all in England now. I sent them there a week ago. I sold my jewels, my all to let them go. I know my children are safe in England. And you, Madame, you are safe with me!"

"Don't call me Madame, call me Louisa."

"And call me Ada," she said.

"So, au revoir!" said Henri. "I shall come round later with your things."

He seized the little girls, and with a nod and "Courage, Louisa," he disappeared.

Oh, the kindness of that broken-hearted Luxemburg woman.

Her poor heart was bleeding for her children, and she kept on weeping, and asking me a thousand questions about England, while she made coffee for me, and spread a white cloth over the kitchen table. What would happen to her little ones? Would the English be kind to them? Would they be safe in England? And over and over again she repeated the same sad little story of how she had sent them away, her three beloveds, George, Clare, and little Ada with the long fair curls; sent them away out of danger, and had never heard a word from them since the day she kissed them and bade them good-bye at the crowded train.

The whole of that day I remained in the kitchen there at the back of the café. I could hear the Germans coming in and out. They were blowing their own trumpets all the time, telling always of their victories.

Ada's little old husband would walk up and down, whistling the cheeriest pipe of a whistle I have ever heard. It did me good to listen to him. It brought before one in the midst of all this terror and ruin an image of birds.

At six o'clock that day, when dusk began to gather, Ada shut up the café, put out the lights, and she and her old husband and I sat together in the kitchen round the fire.

Presently, in came Henri, with my little bag, accompanied by Madame X., and her big husband, and two enormous yellow dogs.

They told me that the Danish Doctor came back at three o'clock, asked for me, and was told I had gone to Holland.

"If it were not for the Danish Doctor I should feel quite safe," I said. "Was he angry?"

"He was very surprised."

"Did he give you back my passport?"

"No."

"Did he get the passport from his Consul?"

"He said so."

"Did he want to know how I got away?"

"He said he hoped you were safe."

"Did he believe you?"

"I don't know."

"Do you *think* he believed you?"

"I don't know."

"Did he *look* as if he believed you?"

"He looked surprised."

"And angry?"

"A little annoyed."

"Not *pleased?*"

"Perhaps!"

"And *very* surprised?"

"Yes, very surprised."

"I don't believe that he believed you."

"Perhaps not."

"Perhaps he will try and find me?"

"But he is no spy," answered Henri. "If he had wanted to betray you he would have done it last night."

"C'est ca!" agreed the others.

"What did you know about him?" I asked. "What made you send him up to me, François? Surely you wouldn't have told him about me unless you *knew* he was trustworthy!"

"C'est ca!" agreed big, fat, sad-eyed Francois. "I have known him for some time. I never doubted him. I am sure he is to be trusted. He has worked very hard among our wounded."

"But why did he speak with the Germans in the restaurant?"

"He is a Dane, he can speak as he choses."

"Then you don't think he was speaking of *me?*"

"No, Madame! C'est evident, n'est-ce-pas? You have left the hotel in safety!"

"Perhaps he will ask Monsieur Claude where I am?"

"Monsieur Claude will tell him he knows nothing about you, has never seen you, never heard of you!"

"Perhaps he will ask Monsieur Claude's sister?"

"We must tell her not to tell him where you are."

"What!"

I started violently.

"Do you mean to say that you haven't warned her already not to tell him where I've really gone to?"

"But of course she will not tell him. She is devoted to you, Madame."

"Call me Louisa."

"Louisa!"

"She might tell him to get rid of him," says Ada slowly.

"C'est ca!" agree the others thoughtfully.

And at that all the terror of last night returns to me. It returns like a *memory*, but it is troublous all the same.

And then, opening my bag to inspect its contents, I suddenly see a big strange key.

What is this?

And then remembrance rushes over me.

It is the key that Mr. Lucien Arthur Jones gave me, the key of the furnished house in Antwerp.

A house! Fully furnished, and fully stored with food! And no occupants! And no Germans! In a flash I decided to get into that house as quickly as possible. It was the best possible place of hiding. It was so good, indeed, that it seemed like a fairy tale that I should have the key in my possession. And then, with another flash, I decided that I could never face going into that house *alone*. My nerves would refuse me. I had asked a good deal of them lately, and they had responded magnificently. But they turned a gainst living alone in an empty house in Antwerp, quite definitely and positively, they turned against that.

Casting a swift glance about me, I took in that group of faces round the kitchen fire. Who were they, these people? Francois, and Lenore, Henri, Ada, and the little old grey-moustached man whistling like a bird, who were they? Why were they here among the Germans? Why had they not fled with the million fugitives. Was it possible they were spies? For I knew now, beyond all doubting, that there were indeed such things as spies, though the English mind finds it almost impossible to believe in the reality of something so dedicated to the gentle art of making melodrama. Until three days ago I had never seen these people in my life. I knew absolutely nothing about them. Perhaps they were even now carefully drawing the net around me. Perhaps I was already a prisoner in the Germans' hands.

And yet they were all I had in the way of aquaintances, they were all I had to trust in.

Could I trust them?

I looked at them again.

It was strange, and rather wonderful, to have nothing on earth to help one but one's own judgment.

Then Ada's voice reached me.

"Voici, Louisa!" she is saying. "Voici le photographie de mon Georges."

And she bends over me with a little old locket, and inside I see a small boy's fair, brave little face, and Ada's tears splash on my hand...

"I sent them away because I feared the Alboches might harm them," she breaks out, uncontrollably. "For mon Mari and myself, we have no fear! And we had not money for ourselves to go. But my Georges, and my Clare, and my petite Ada – I could not bear the thought that the Alboches might hurt them. Oh, mes petites, mes petites! They wept so. They did not want to go. ' Let us stay here with you, Mama. ' But I made them go. I sold my bjoux, my all, to get money enough for them to go to England. Oh, the English will be good 'to them, won't they, Louisa? Tell me the English will be good to my petites."

Sometimes, in England since, when I have heard some querulous suburban English heart voicing itself grandiloquently, out of the plethora of its charity-giving, as "*a bit fed up with the refugees*" I think of myself, with a passionate sincerity and fanatic belief in England's goodness and justice, assuring that weeping mother that her Georges and Clare and little Ada with the long hair curls would be cared for by the English – the tender, generous, grateful English – as though they were their own little ones – even better perhaps, even better! Ada's tears!

They wash away my fears. My heart melts to her, and I tell her straightway about the house in the avenue L.

"But how splendid!" she cries exuberantly.

"Quel chance, Louisa, quel chance!" cries Lenore.

"To-morrow morning we shall all take you there!" declares Henri.

Their surprise, their delight, allay my last lingering doubts.

"But mind," I urge them feverishly, "You must never let the Danish Doctor know that address."

That night I sleep in a feather-bed in a room at the top of dear Ada's house.

Or try to sleep! Alas, it is only trying. My windows look on a long narrow street, a dead street, full of empty houses, and from these houses come stealing with louder and louder insistence the sounds of those imprisoned dogs howling within the barred doors of the empty houses. Their cries are terrible, they are starving now and perishing of thirst. They yelp and whine, and wail, they bark and shriek and plead, they sob, they moan. They send forth blood-curdling cries, in dozens, in hundreds, from every street, from every quarter, these massed wails go up into the night, lending a new horror to the dark.

And through it all the Germans sleep, they make no attempt either to destroy the poor tortured brutes, or to give them food and water, they are to be left there to die. Hour after hour goes by, I bury my head under a pillow, but I cannot shut out those awful sounds, they penetrate through everything, sometimes they are death-agonies; the dogs are giving up, they can suffer no longer. They understand at last that mankind, their friend, who has had all their faith and love, has deserted them, and then with fresh bursts of howling they seem afresh to make him listen, to make him realize this dark and terrible thing that has come to them, this racking thirst and hunger that he has been so careful to provide against before, even as though they were his children, his own little ones, not his dogs. And, they howl, and cry, the dead city listens, and gives no sign, and they shiver, and shriek, and wail, but in vain, in vain. It is the most awful night of my life!

CHAPTER XLV

A SAFE SHELTER

Next morning at ten o'clock, Lenore and I and the ever-faithful Henri (carrying my parrot, if you please) and Ada strolled with affected nonchalance through the Antwerp streets where a pale gold sun was shining on the ruins.

Germans were everywhere. Some were buying postcards, some sausages. Motor cars dashed in and out full of grey or blue uniforms. Fair, grave, sardonic faces were to be seen now, where only a few brief days ago there had been naught but Belgians' brave eyes, and lively, tender physiognomy. Our little party was silent, depressed. I wore a handkerchief over my head, tied beneath my chin, a big black apron, and a white shawl, and I kept my arm inside Henri's.

"Voici, Madame," he exclaimed suddenly. "Voila les Anglais."

"Et les Anglaises," gasped Ada under her breath.

We were just then crossing the Avenue de Kaiser – that once gay, bright Belgian Avenue where I had so often walked with Alice, my dear little *Liégeoise*, now fled, alas, I knew not where.

A procession was passing between the long lines of fading acacias. A huge waggon, some mounted Germans, two women.

"Oh, mon Dieu!" says Ada.

Lying on sacks in the open waggon are wounded English officers, their eyes shut.

And trudging on foot behind the waggon, with an indescribable steadfastness and courage, is an English nurse in her blue uniform, and a tall, thin, erect English lady, with grey hair and a sweet face under a wide black hat.

"They are taking them to Germany!" whispers Henri in my ear.

"Mon Dieu, mon Dieu!" moans Ada under her breath. "Oh, les pauvres Anglaises!"

It was all I could do to keep from flying towards them.

An awful longing came over me to speak to them, to sympathise, to do something, anything to help them, there alone among the Germans. It was the call of one's race, of one's blood, of one's country. But it was madness. I must stand still. To speak to them might mean bad things for all of us.

And even as I thought of that, the group vanished round the corner, towards the station.

As we walked along we examined the City. Ah, how shocking was the change! People are wont to say of Antwerp that it was very little damaged. But in truth it suffered horribly, far beyond what anyone who has not seen it can believe. The burning streets were still on fire. The water supply was still cut off. The burning had continued ever since the bombardment. I looked at the Hotel St. Antoine and shivered. A few days ago Sir Frederick Greville and Lady Greville of the British Embassy had been installed in that hotel and countless Belgian Ministers. The Germans had tried hard to shell it, but their shells had fallen across the road instead. All the opposite side of the street lay flat on the ground, smouldering, and smoking, in heaps of spread-out burning ruins.

At last we reached the house for which I had the key.

From the outside it was dignified, handsome, thoroughly Belgian, standing in a street of many ruined houses.

Trembling, I put the key into the lock, turned it, and pushed open the door. Then I gasped. "Open Sesame" indeed! For there, stretching before me, was a magnificent hall, richly carpeted, with broad, low marble stairs leading upwards on either side to strangely-constructed open apartments lined with rare books, and china, and silver. We crept in, and shut the door behind us. Moving about the luxurious rooms and corridors, with bated breath, on tip-toe we explored. No fairy tale could reveal greater wonders. Here was a superb mansion stocked for six months' siege! In the cellars were huge cases of white wines, and red wines, and mineral waters galore. In the pantries we found hundreds of tins of sardines, salmon, herrings, beef, mutton, asparagus, corn, and huge bags of flour, boxes of biscuits, boxes of salt, sugar, pepper, porridge, jams, potatoes. At the back was a garden, full of great trees, and grass, and flowers, with white roses on the rose-bush.

Agreeable as was the sight, there was yet something infinitely touching in this beautiful silent home, deserted by its owners, who, secure in the impregnability of Antwerp, had provided themselves for a six months' siege, and then, at the last moment, their hopes crushed, had fled, leaving furniture, clothes, food, wines, everything, just for dear life's sake.

Tender-hearted Ada wept continually as she moved about.

"Oh, the poor thing!" she sighed every now and then. And forgetting herself and her own grief, her angel heart would overflow with compassion for these people whom she had never seen, never heard of until now.

For the first time for days I felt safe, and when Lenore (Madame X.) and her husband promised to come and stay there with me, and bring Jeanette and the old grandmere from the hospital I was greatly relieved. In fact if it had not been for the Danish Doctor I should have been quite happy.

They all came in that afternoon, and Henri too, and how grateful they were to get into that nest.

We quickly decided to use only the kitchen, and Lenore and her husband shewed such a respect for the beauties of the house, that I knew I had done right in bringing the poor refugees here.

Through the barred kitchen windows, from behind the window curtains, we watched the endless rush of the German machinery. Occasionally Germans would come and knock at the door, and Lenore would go and answer it. When they found the house was occupied they immediately went away.

So I had the satisfaction of knowing that I was saving that house from the Huns.

The haunted noontide silence of my solitary walk seemed like a dream now. Noise without end went on. All day long the Germans were rushing their machineries through the Chausee de Malines, or Rue Lamariniere, or along the Avenue de Kaiser. At some of the monsters that went grinding along one stared, gasping, realising for the first time what *les petits Belges* had been up against when they had pitted courage and honour and love of liberty against machinery like that. Three days afterwards along the road from Lierre two big guns moved on locomotives towards Aerschot, suggesting by their vastness that immense mountain peaks were journeying across a landscape. I felt physically ill when I saw the size of them. A hundred and fifty portable kitchens ensconced in motor cars also passed through the town, explaining practically why all the Germans look so remarkably well-fed. Motor cycles fitted with wireless telegraphy, motor loads of boats in sections, air-sheds in sections, and trams in sections dashed by eternally. The swift rush of motor cars seemed never to end.

Yet, busy as the Germans were, and feverishly concentrated on their new activities, they still found time to carry out their system as applied to their endeavours to win the Belgian people's confidence in their kindness and justice as Conquerers! They paid for everything they bought, food, lodging, drink, everything. They asked for things gently, even humbly. They never grumbled if they were kept waiting. They patted the children's heads. Over and over again I heard them saying the same thing to anybody who would listen.

"We love you Belgians! We *know* how brave you are. We only want-ed to go through Belgium. We would never have hurt it. And we would have paid you for any damage we did. We don't hate the French either. They are '*bons soldats,*' the French! But the '*Englisch*' (and here a positive hiss of hatred would come into their guttural voices), the '*Englisch*' are false to *everyone*. It was they who made the war. It is all their fault, whatever has happened. We didn't want this war. We did all we could to stop it. But the '*Englisch*' (again the hiss of hatred, ringing like cold steel through the word) wanted to fight us, they were jealous of us, and they used you poor brave Belgians as an excuse!"

That was always the beginning of their Litany.

Then they would follow the Chant of their victories.

"And now we are going to Calais! We shall start the bombardment of England from there with our big guns. Before long we shall all be in London."

And then would come the final strain, which was often true, as a matter of fact, in addition to being wily.

"I've left my good home behind me and my dear good wife, and away there in the Vaterland I have seven children awaiting my return. So you can imagine if *I* and men like me, wanted this war!"

It was generally seven children.

Sometimes it was more.

But it was never less!

The system was perfect, even about as small a thing as that!

CHAPTER XLVI

THE FLIGHT INTO HOLLAND

For five wild incredible days I remained in Antwerp, watching the German occupation; and then at last, I found my opportunity to escape over the borders into Holland.

There came the great day when François managed to borrow a motor car and took me out through the Breda Gate to Putte in Holland.

Good-bye to Ada, good-bye to Henri, good-bye to Lenore, Jeannette and la grandmère!

I knew now that Madame X. could be trusted to the death. She had proved it in an unmistakable way. In my bag I had her Belgian passport and her German one also. I was passing now as François' wife. The photograph of Lenore stamped on the passport was sufficiently like myself to enable me to pass the German sentinels, and Lenore, dear, sweet, lovable Lenore, had coached me diligently in the pronunciation of her queer Flemish name – which was *not* Lenore, of course.

As for my own English passport, Monsieur X. went several times to the young Danish Doctor asking for it on my behalf.

The Dane refused to give it up. "How do I know," said he, "that you will restore it to the lady?"

Finally Monsieur X. suggested that he should leave it for me at the American Consulate.

Eventually, long after it came to me in London from the American Consulate, with a note from the Dane asking them to see that I got it safely.

When I think of it now, I feel sad to have so mistrusted that friendly Dane. What did he think, I wonder, to find me suddenly flown? Perhaps he will read this some day, and understand, and forgive.

Ah, how mournful, how heart-breaking was the almost incredible change that had taken place in the free, happy country of former days and this ruined desolate land of to-day. As we flashed along towards Holland we passed endless burnt-out villages and farms, magnificent old chateaux shelled to the ground, churches lying tumbled forward upon their graveyards, tombstones uprooted and graves riven open. A cold wind blew; the sky was grey and sad; in all the melancholy and chill there was one thought and one alone that made these sights endurable. It was that the poor victims of these horrors were being cared for and comforted in England's and Holland's big warm hearts.

I could scarcely believe my eyes when I saw on the Dutch borders those sweet green Dutch pine-woods of Putte stretching away under the peaceful golden evening skies. Trees! *Trees!* Were there really such things left in the world? It seemed impossible that any beauty could be still in existence; and I gazed at the woods with ravenous eyes, drinking in their beauty and peace like a perishing man slaking his thirst in clear cold water.

Then, suddenly, out of the depths of those dim Dutch woods, I discerned white faces peering, and presently I became aware that the woods were alive with human beings. White gaunt faces, looked out from behind the tree-trunks, faces of little frightened children, peeping, peering, wondering, faces of sad, hopeless men, gazing stonily, faces of hollow-eyed women who had turned grey with anguish when that cruel hail of shells began to burst upon their little homes in Antwerp, drawing them in their terror out into the unknown,

Right through the woods of Putte ran the road to the city of Berg-op-Zoom, and along this road I saw a huge military car come flying, manned by half a dozen Dutch Officers and laden with thousands of loaves of bread. Instantly, out of the woods, out of their secret lairs, the poor homeless fugitives rushed forward, gathering round the car, holding out their hands in a passion of supplication, and whispering hoarsely, "Du pain! Du pain!" Bread! Bread!

It was like a scene from Dante, the white faces, the outstretched arms, the sunset above the wood, and the red camp fires between the trees.

CHAPTER XLVII

FRIENDLY HOLLAND

Yesterday I was in Holland.

To-day I am in England.

But still in my ears I can hear the ring of scathing indignation in the voices of all those innumerable Dutch when I put point-blank to them the question that has been causing such unrest in Great Britain lately: "Are the Dutch helping Germany?"

From every sort and condition of Dutchmen I received an emphatic "never!" The people of Holland would never permit it, and in Holland the people have an enormous voice. Nothing could have been more emphatic or more convincing than that reply. But I pressed the point further. "Is it not true, then, that the Dutch allowed German troops to pass through Holland?"

The answer I received was startling.

"We have heard that story. And we cannot understand how the Allies could believe it. We have traced the story," my informant went on, "to its origin and we have discovered that the report was circulated by the Germans themselves."

I pressed my interrogation further still.

"Would it be correct, then, to say that the attitude of Holland towards England is distinctly and unmistakably friendly among all sections of the community in Holland?"

My informant, one of the best known of Dutch advocates, paused a moment before replying.

Then seriously and deliberately he made the following statement: –

"In the upper circles of Dutch Society – that is to say, in Court circles and in the military set that is included in this classification – there has been, it is true, a somewhat sentimental partiality for Germany and the Germans. This preference originated obviously from Prince Henry's nationality, and from Queen Wilhelmina's somewhat passive acceptance of her husband's likes and dislikes. But the situation has lately changed. A new emotion has seized upon Holland, and one of the first to be affected by this new emotion was Prince Henry himself. When the million Belgian refugees, bleeding, starving, desperate, hunted, flung themselves over the Dutch border in the agony of their flight, we Dutch – and Prince Henry among us – saw for ourselves for the first time the awful horror of the German invasion."

"And so the Prince has shewed himself sympathetic towards the Allies?"

"He has devoted himself to the Belgian Cause," was the reply. "Day after day he has taken long journeys to all the Dutch cities and villages where the refugees are congregated. He has visited the hospitals everywhere. He has made endless gifts. In the hospitals, by his geniality and simplicity he completely overcame the quite natural shrinking of the wounded Belgian soldiers from a visitor who bore the hated name of German."

I knew it was true, too, because I had myself seen Prince Henry going in and out of the hospitals at Bergen-op-Zoom, his face wearing an expression of deep commiseration.

"But what about England?" I went on hurriedly. "How do you feel to us?"

"We are your friends," came the answer. "What puzzles us is how England could ever doubt or misunderstand us on that point. Psychologically, we feel ourselves more akin to England than to any other country. We like the English ways, which greatly resemble our own. Just as much as we like English manners and customs, we dislike the manners and customs of Germany. That we should fight against England is absolutely unthinkable. In fact it would mean one thing only, in Holland – a revolution."

Over and over again these opinions were presented to me by leading Dutchmen.

A director of a big Dutch line'of steamers was even more emphatic concerning Holland's attitude to England.

"And we are," he said, "suffering from the War in Holland – suffering badly. We estimate our losses at 60 per cent, of our ordinary trade and commerce."

He pointed out to me a paragraph in a Dutch paper.

"If the export prohibition by Britain of wool, worsted, etc., is maintained, the manufactures of woollen stuffs here will within not a very long period, perhaps five to six weeks, have to be closed for lack of raw material."

"A proposition of the big manufacturers to have the prohibition raised on condition that nothing should be delivered to Germany is being submitted to the British Government. We hope that England will arrive at a favourable decision."

"You know," I said tentatively, "that rumour persists in attributing to Holland a readiness to do business with Germany?"

"Let me be quite frank about that," said the director thoughtfully. "It is true that some people have surreptitiously been doing business with Germany. But in every community you will find that sort of people. But our Government has now awakened to the treachery, and we shall hear no more of such transactions in the future."

"And is it true that you are trying to change your national flag because the Germans have been misusing it?"

"It is quite true. We are trying to adopt the ancient standard of Holland – the orange – instead of the red, white and blue of to-day."

As an earnest of the genuine sympathy felt by the Dutch as a whole towards the Belgian sufferers I may describe in a few words what I saw in Holland.

Out of the black horrors of Antwerp, out of the hell of bombs and shells, these million people came fleeing for their lives into Dutch territory. Penniless, footsore, bleeding, broken with terror and grief, dying in hundreds by the way, the inhabitants of Antwerp and its villages crushed blindly onwards till they reached the Dutch frontiers, where they flung themselves, a million people, on the pity and mercy of Holland, not knowing the least how they would be treated. And what did Holland do? With a magnificent simplicity, she opened her arms as no nation in the history of the world has ever opened its arms yet to strangers, and she took the whole of those million stricken creatures to her heart.

The Dutch at Bergen-op-Zoom, where the majority of the refugees were gathered, gave up every available building to these people. They filled all their churches with straw to make beds for them; they opened all their theatres, their schools, their hospitals, their factories and their private homes, and, without a murmur, indeed, with a tenderness and gentleness beyond all description, they took upon their shoulders the burden of these million victims of Germany's brutality.

"It is our duty," they say quietly; and sick and poor alike pour out their offerings graciously, without ceasing.

In the Grand Place of Bergen-op-Zoom stand long lines of soup-boilers over charcoal fires.

Behind the line of soup-boilers are stacks of bones, hundreds of bags of rice and salt, mountains of celery and onions, all piled on the flags of the market-place, while to add to the liveliness and picturesqueness of the scene, Dutch soldiers in dark blue and yellow uniforms ride slowly round the square on glossy brown horses, keeping the thousands of refugees out of the way of the endless stream of motor cars lining the Grand Place on its four sides, all packed to the brim with bread, meat, milk, and cheese.

Inside the Town hall the portrait of Queen Wilhelmina in her scarlet and ermine robes looks down on the strangest scene Holland has seen for many a day.

The floors of the Hotel de la Ville are covered with thousands of big red Dutch cheeses. Twenty-six thousand kilos of long loaves of brown bread are packed up almost to the ceiling, looking exactly like enormous wood stacks. Sacks of flour, sides of pork and bacon, cases of preserved meat and conserved milk, hundreds of cans of milk, piles of blankets, piles of clothing are here also, all to be given away.

The town of Bergen-op-Zoom is full of heartbreaking pictures to-day, but to me the most pathetic of all is the writing on the walls.

It is a tremendous tribute to the good-heartedness of the Dutch that they do not mind their scrupulously clean houses defaced for the moment in this way.

Scribbled in white chalk all over the walls, shutters, and fences, windows, tree-trunks, and pavements, are the addresses of the frenzied refugees, trying to get in touch with their lost relations.

On the trees, too, little bits of paper are pinned, covered with addresses and messages, such as "The Family Montchier can be found in the Church of St. Joseph under the grand altar," or "Anna Decart with Pierre and Marie and Grandmother are in the School of Music.""Les sœurs Martell et Grandmere are in the Church of the Holy Martyrs.""La Famille Deminn are in the fifth tent of the encampment on the Artillery ground." "M. and Mme. Ardige and their seven children are in the Comedy Theatre."... So closely are the walls and shutters and the windows and trees scribbled over by now that the million addresses are most of them becoming indistinguishable.

While I was in Holland I came across an interesting couple whom I speedily classified in my own mind.

One was a dark young man.

He had a peculiar accent. He told me he was an Englishman from Northampton.

Perhaps he was.

He said the reason he wasn't fighting for his country was because he was too fat.

Perhaps he was.

The other young man said he was American.

Perhaps he was.

He had red hair and an American accent. He had lived in Germany a great deal in his childhood.

All went well until the red-haired man made the following curious slip.

When I was describing the way the Germans in Antwerp fled towards the sausage, he said, "How they will roar when I tell them that in Berlin!"

Swiftly he corrected himself.

"In New York, I mean!" he said.

But a couple of hours later the Englishman left suddenly for London, and the American left for Antwerp. As I had happened to mention that I had left my baggage in Antwerp, I could quite imagine it being overhauled by the Germans there, at the instigation of the red-haired young gentleman with the pronounced American accent.

A rough estimate of the cost to the Dutch Government of maintaining the refugees works out at something like £85,000 a week. This, of course, is quite irrespective of the boundless private hospitality which is being dispensed with the utmost generosity on every hand in Rotterdam, Haarlem, Flushing, Bergen-op-Zoom, Maasstricht, Rossendal, Delft, and innumerable other towns and villages.

Some of the military families on their meagre pay must find the call on them a severe strain, but one never hears of complaints on this score, and in nine cases out of ten they refuse absolutely to accept payment for board and lodging, though many of the refugees are eager to pay for their food and shelter.

"We can't make money out of them!" is what the Dutch say. A new reading this, of the famous couplet of a century ago: –

In matters of this kind the fault of the Dutch,
Was giving too little and asking too much.

PART II

CHAPTER XLVIII

FRENCH COOKING IN WAR TIME

There is no more Belgium to go to.

So I am in France now.

But War-Correspondents are not wanted here. They are driven out wherever discovered. I shall not stay long.

All my time is taken up in running about getting papers; my bag is getting out of shape; it bulges with the Liasser Passers, and Sauf Conduits that one has to fight so hard to get.

However, to be among French-speaking people again is a great joy.

And to-day in Dunkirk it has refreshed and consoled me greatly to see Madame Piers cooking.

The old Frenchwoman moved about her tiny kitchen, – her infinitesimally tiny kitchen, – and I watched her from my point of observation, seated on a tiny chair, at a tiny table, squeezed up into a tiny corner.

It really was the smallest kitchen I'd ever seen. No, you couldn't have swung a cat in it – you really couldn't.

And no one but a thrifty French housewife could have contrived to get that wee round table and little chair into that tiny angle.

Yet I felt very cosy and comfortable there, and the old grey-haired French mother, preparing supper for her household, and for any soldier who might be passing by, seemed perfectly satisfied with her cramped surroundings, and kept begging me graciously to remain where I was, drinking the hot tea she had just made for me, while my boots (that were always wet out there) dried under her big charcoal stove. And always she smiled away; and I smiled too. Who could help it?

She and her kitchen were the most charming study imaginable.

Every now and then her fine, old, brown, thin, wrinkled hand would reach over my head for a pot, or a brush, or a pan, from the wall behind, or the shelf above me, while the other hand would stir or shake something over the wee gas-ring or the charcoal stove. For so small was the kitchen that by stretching she could reach at the same time to the wall on either side.

Then she began to pick over a pile of rough-looking green stuff, very much like that we in England should contemptuously call weeds.

Pick, pick, pick!

A diamond merchant with his jewels could not have been more careful, more delicate, more watchful. And as I thought that, it suddenly came over me that to this old, careful, thrifty Frenchwoman those weedy greens were not weeds at all, but were really as precious as diamonds, for she was a Frenchwoman, clever and disciplined in the art of thrift, and they represented the most important thing in all the world to-day – food.

Food means life.

Food means victory.

Food means the end of the War, and PEACE.

You could read all that in her black, intelligent eyes.

Then I began to sit up and watch her more closely still.

When she had picked off all those little hard leaves, she cracked up the bare, harsh stalks into pieces an inch long, and flung them all, leaves and stalks, into a saucepan of boiling water, which she presently pushed aside to let simmer away gently for ten minutes or so.

Meanwhile she is carefully pealing a hard-boiled egg, taking the shell off in two pieces, and shredding up the white on a little white saucer, never losing a crumb of it even.

An egg! Why waste an egg like that? But indeed, she is not going to waste it. She is using the yolk to make mayonnaise sauce, and the white is for decoration later on. With all her thrift she must have things pretty. Her cheap dishes must have an air of finish, an artistic touch; and she knows, and acts up to the fact, that the yellow and white egg is not wasted, but returns a hundred per cent., because it is going to make her supper look a hundred times more important than it really is.

Now she takes the greens from the saucepan, drains them, and puts them into a little frying-pan on the big stove; and she peppers and salts them, and turns them about, and leaves them with a little smile.

She always has that little smile for everything, and I think that goes into the flavour somehow!

And now she pours the water the greens were boiled in, into that big soup-pot on the big stove, and gives the soup a friendly stir just to shew that she hasn't forgotten it.

She opens the cupboard, and brings out every little or big bit of bread left over from lunch and breakfast, and she shapes them a little with her sharp old knife, and she hurries them all into the big pot, putting the lid down quickly so that even the steam doesn't get out and get wasted!

Now she takes the greens off the fire, and puts them into a dear little round white china dish, and leaves them to get cold.

She opens her cupboard again and brings out a piece of cold veal cutlet and a piece of cold steak left over from luncheon yesterday, and to-day also. What is she going to do with these? She is going to make them our special dish for supper. She begins to shred them up with her old sharp blade – shreds them up finely, not mincing, not chopping, but shredding the particles apart – and into them she shreds a little cold ham and onion, and then she flavours it well with salt and pepper. Then she piles this all on a dish and covers it with golden mayonnaise, and criss-crosses it with long red wires of beetroot.

The greens are cold now, and she dresses them. She oils them, and vinegars them, and pats and arranges them, and decorates them with the white of the chopped egg and thin little slices of tomato.

"Voila! The salad!" she says, with her flash of a smile.

Salad for five people – a beautiful, tasty, green, melting, delicious salad that might have been made of young asparagus tips! And what did it cost? One farthing, plus the labour and care and affection and time that the old woman put into the making of it – plus, in other words, her thrift!

Now she must empty my teapot.

Does she turn it upside down over a bucket of rubbish as they do in England, leaving the tea-leaves to go to the dustman when he calls on Friday?

She would think that an absolutely wicked thing to do if she had ever heard of such proceedings, but she has not.

She drains every drop of tea into a jug, puts a lid on it, and places it away in her safe; then she empties the tea-leaves into a yellow earthenware basin, and puts a plate over them, and puts them up on a shelf.

I begin to say to myself, with quite an excited feeling, "Shall I ever see her throw anything away?"

Potatoes next.

Ah! Now there'll be peelings, and those she'll have to throw away.

Not a bit of it!

There are only the very thinnest, filmiest scrapings of dark down off this old dear's potatoes. And suddenly I think of poor dear England, where our potato skins are so thick that a tradition has grown from them, and the maids throw them over their shoulders and see what letter they make on the floor, and that will be the first letter of *his* name! Laughing, I tell of this tradition to my old Frenchwoman.

And what do you think she answers?

"The skin must be very thick not to break," she says solemnly." But then you English are all so rich!"

Are we?

Or are we simply – what?

Is it that, bluntly put, we are lazy?

After the fall of Antwerp, when a million people had fled into

Holland, I saw ladies in furs and jewels holding up beseeching, imploring hands to the kindly but bewildered Dutch folk asking for bread – just bread! It was a terrible sight! But shall we, too, be begging for bread some day? Shall we, too, be longing for the pieces we threw away? Who knows?

Finally we sat down to an exquisite supper.

First, there was croûte au pot – the nicest soup in the world, said a King of France, and full of nourishment.

Then there was a small slice each of tender, juicy boiled beef out of the big soup-pot, never betraying for a minute that that beautiful soup had been made from it.

With that beef went the potatoes sautee in butter, and sprinkled with chopped green.

After that came the chicken mayonnaise and salad of asparagus tips (otherwise cold scraps and weeds).

There are five of us to supper in that little room behind the milliner's shop – an invalided Belgian officer; a little woman from Malines looking after her wounded husband in hospital here; Mdlle. Alice, the daughter, who keeps the millinery shop in the front room; the old mother, a high lace collar on now, and her grey hair curled and coiffured; and myself. The mother waits on us, slipping in and out like a cat, and we eat till there is nothing left to want, and nothing left to eat. And then we have coffee – such coffee!

Which reminds me that I quite forgot to say I caught the old lady putting the shells of the hard-boiled egg into the coffee-pot!

And that is French cooking in War time!

CHAPTER XLIX

THE FIGHT IN THE AIR

Next morning, Sunday, about half-past ten, I was walking joyfully on that long, beautiful beach at Dunkirk, with all the winds in the world in my face, and a golden sun shining dazzlingly over the blue skies into the deep blue sea-fields beneath.

The rain had ceased. The peace of God was drifting down like a dove's wing over the tortured world. From the city of Dunkirk a mile beyond the Plage the chimes of Sabbath bells stole out soothingly, and little black-robed Frenchwomen passed with prayer books and eyes down bent.

It was Sunday morning, and for the first time in this new year religion and spring were met in the golden beauty of a day that was windswept and sunlit simultaneously, and that swept away like magic the sad depression of endless grey monotonous days of rain and mud.

And then, all suddenly, a change came sweeping over the golden beach and the turquoise skies overhead and all the fair glory of the glittering morning turned with a crash into tragedy.

Crash! Crash!

Bewildered, not understanding, I heard one deafening intonation after another fling itself fiercely from the cannons that guard the port and city of Dunkirk.

Then followed the shouts of fishermen, soldiers, nurses and the motley handful of people who happened to be on the beach just then.

Everybody began shouting and everybody began running and

pointing towards the sky; and then I saw the commencement of the most extraordinary sight this war has witnessed.

An English aeroplane was chasing a German Taube that had suddenly appeared above the coast-lime. The German was doing his best to make a rush for Dunkirk, and the Englishman was doing his best to stop him. As I watched I held my breath.

The English aeroplane came on fiercely and mounted with a swift rush till it gained a place in the bright blue skies above the little insect-like Taube.[10]

It seemed that the English aviator must now get the better of his foe; but suddenly, with an incredible swiftness, the German doubled and, giving up his attempt to get across the city, fled eastwards like a mad thing, with the Englishman after him.

But now one saw that the German machine responded more quickly and had far the better of it as regards pace, leaving the pursuing Englishman soon far behind it, and rushing away across the skies at a really incredible rate.

But while this little thrilling byplay was engaging the attention of everyone far greater things were getting in train.

Another Taube was sneaking, unobserved, among the clouds, and was rapidly gaining a place high up above Dunkirk.

And now it lets fall a bomb, that drops down, down, into the town beneath.

Immediately, with a sound like the splitting of a million worlds, everything and everyone opens fire, French, English, Belgians, and all.

The whole earth seems to have gone mad. Up into the sky they are all firing, up into the brilliant golden sunlight at that little black, swiftly-moving creature, that spits out venomously every two or three minutes black bombs that go slitting through the air with a faint

---

[10] The Etrich Taube ("taube" is the German for "dove") was a monoplan aircraft designed in 1909 in Austria-Hungary and used at the beginning of war by the Air Forces of Germany, Austria and Italy.

screech till they touch the earth and shed death and destruction all around.

And now – what's this?

All along the shore, slipping and sailing along across the sky comes into sight an endless succession of Taubes.

They glitter like silver in the sunlight, defying all the efforts of the French artillery; they sail along with a calm insouciance that nearly drives me mad.

Crash! crash! crash! Bang! bang! bang! The cannon and the rifles are at them now with a fury that defies all words.

The firing comes from all directions. They are firing inland and they are firing out to sea. At last I run into a house with some French soldiers who are clenching their hands with rage at that Taube's behaviour.

One! two! three! four! five! six! seven! eight! nine! ten!

Everyone is counting.

Eleven! twelve! thirteen! fourteen! fifteen! sixteen!

"Voila au autre!" cry the French soldiers every minute.

They utter groans of rage and disgust.

The glittering cavalcade sails serenely onward, until the whole sky-line from right to left above the beach is dotted with those sparkling creatures, now outlined against the deep plentiful blue of the sky, and now gliding and hiding beneath some vast soft drift of feathery grey-white cloud.

It is a sight never to be forgotten. Its beauty is so vivid, so thrilling, that it is difficult to realise that this lovely spectacle of a race across the sky is no game, no race, no exhibition, but represents the ultimate end of all the races and prizes and exhibitions and attempts to fly. Here is the whole art of flying in a tabloid as it were, with all its significance at last in evidence.

The silver aeroplanes over the sea keep guard 'all the time, moving along very, very slowly, and very high up, until the Taube has dropped its last bomb over the city.

Then they glide away across the sea in the direction of England.

I walked back to the city. What a change since I came through it an hour or so before! I looked at the Hotel de Ville and shuddered.

All the windows were smashed; and just at the side, in a tiny green square, was the great hole that showed where the bomb had fallen harmlessly.

All the afternoon the audacious Taube remained rushing about high above Dunkirk.

But later that afternoon, as I was in a train en route for Furnes, fate threw in my way the chance to see a glorious vindication!

The train was brought suddenly to a standstill. We all jumped up and looked out.

It was getting dusk, but against the red in the sky two black things were visible.

One dropped a bomb, intended for the railway station a little further on.

By that we knew it was German, but we had little time to think.

The other aeroplane rushed onwards; firing was heard, and down came the German, followed by the Frenchman.

They alighted almost side by side.

We could see quite plainly men getting out and rushing towards each other.

A few minutes later some peasants came rushing to tell us that the two Germans from the Taube both lay dead on the edge of that sandy field to westward.

Then our train went on.

CHAPTER L

THE WAR BRIDE

The train went on.

It was dark, quite dark, when I got out of it at last, and looked about me blinking.

This was right at the Front in Flanders, and a long cavalcade of French soldiers were alighting also.

Two handsome elderly Turcos with splendid eyes, black beards, and strange, hard, warrior-like faces, passed, looking immensely distinguished as they mounted their arab horses, and rode off into the night, swathed in their white head-dresses, with their flowing picturesque cloaks spread out over their horses' tails, their swords clanking at their sides, and their blazing eyes full of queer, bold pride.

Then, to my great surprise, I see coming out of the station two ladies wrapped in furs, a young lady and an old one.

"Delightful," I think to myself.

As I come up with them I hear them enquiring of a sentinel the way to the Hotel de Noble Rose, and with the swift friendliness of War time I stop and ask if I may walk along with them.

"Je suis Anglais!" I add.

"Avec beaucoup de plaisir!" they cry simultaneously.

"We are just arrived from Folkestone," the younger one explains in pretty broken English, as we grope our way along the pitch-black cobbled road. "Ah! But what a journey!"

But her voice bubbles as she speaks, and, though I cannot see her face, I suddenly become aware that for some reason or other this girl is filled with quite extraordinary happiness.

Picking our way along the road in the dark, with the cannons growling away fiercely some six miles off, she tells me her "petite histoire."

She is a little Brussels bride, in search of her soldier bridegroom, and she has, by dint of persistent, never-ceasing coaxing, persuaded her old mother to set out from Brussels, all this long, long way, through Antwerp, to Holland, then to Flushing, then to Folkestone, then to Calais, then to Dunkirk, and finally here, to the Front, where her soldier bridegroom will be found. He is here. He has been wounded. He is better. He has always said, "No! no! you must not come." And now at last he had said, "Come," and here she is!

She is so pretty, so simple, so girlish, and sweet, and the mother is such a perfect old duck of a mother, that I fall in love with them both.

Presently we find ourselves in the quaint old Flemish Inn with oil lamps and dark beams.

The stout, grey-moustached landlord hastens forward.

"Have you a message for Madame Louis." The bride gasps out her question.

"Oui, Oui, Madame!" the landlord answers heartily. "There is a message for you. You are to wait here. That is the message!"

"Bien!"

Her eyes flame with joy.

So we order coffee and sit at a little table, chattering away. But I confess that all I want is to watch that young girl's pale, dark face.

Rays of light keep illuminating it, making it almost divinely beautiful, and it seems to me I have never come so close before to another human being's joy.

And then a soldier walks in.

He comes towards her. She springs to her feet.

He utters a word.

He is telling her her husband is out in the passage.

Very wonderful is the way that girl gets across the big, smoky, Flemish cafe.

I declare she scarcely touches the ground. It is as near flying as anyone human could come. Then she is through the door, and we see no more.

Ah, but we can imagine it, we two, the old mother and I!

And we look at each other, and her eyes are wet, and so are mine, and we smile, but very mistily, very shakily, at the thought of those two in the little narrow passage outside, clasped in each others' arms.

* * * *

They come in presently.

They sit with us now, the dear things, sit hand in hand, and their young faces are almost too sacred to look at, so dazzling is the joy written in both his and hers.

They are bathed in smiles that keep breaking over their lips and eyes like sunkissed breakers on a summer strand, and everything they say ends in a broken laugh.

And then we go into dinner, and they make me dine with them, and they order red wine, and make me have some, and I cease to be a stranger, I become an old friend, intermingling with that glorious happiness which seems to be mine as well as theirs because they are lovers and love all the world.

The old mother whispers to me sottly when she got a chance: "He will be so pleased when he knows! There's a little one coming."

"Oh, wonderful little one!" I whisper back.

She understands and nods between tears and smiles again, while the two divine ones sit gazing at the paradise in each other's eyes.

And through it all, all the time, goes on the hungry growl of cannons, and just a few miles out continue, all the time, those wild and passionate struggles for life and death between the Allies and Germans, which soon – God in His mercy forbid – may fling this smiling, fair-headed boy out into the sad dark glory of death on the battlefield, leaving his little one fatherless.

Ah, but with what a heritage!

And then, all suddenly, I think to myself, who would not be glad and proud to come to life under such Epic Happenings. Such glorious heroic beginnings, with all that is commonplace and worldly left out, and all that is stirring and deep and vital put in.

* * * *

Never in the history of the world have there been as many marriages as now. Everywhere girls and men are marrying. No longer do they hesitate, and ponder, and hang back. Instead they rush towards each other, eagerly, confidentially, right into each others' arms, into each others' lives.

"Till Death us do part!" say those thousands of brave young voices.

Indeed it seems to me that never in the history of this old, old world was love as wonderful as now. Each bride is a heroine, and oh, the hero that every bridegroom is! They snatch at happiness. They discover now, in one swift instant, what philosophers have spent years in teaching – that "life is fleeting," and they are afraid to lose one of the golden moments which may so soon come to an end for ever.

But that is not all.

There is something else behind it all – something no less beautiful, though less personal.

There is the intention of the race to survive.

Consciously, sometimes, – but more often unconsciously – our men and our women are mating for the sake of the generation that will follow, the children who will rise up and call them blessed, the brave, strong, wonderful children, begotten of brave, sweet women who joyously took all risks, and splendid, heroic men with hearts soft with love and pity for the women they left behind, but with iron determination steeling their souls to fight to the death for their country.

How superb will be the coming generation, begotten under such glorious circumstances, with nothing missing from their magnificent heritage, Love, Patriotism, Courage, Devotion, Sacrifice, Death, and Glory!

* * * *

A week after that meeting at the Front I was in Dunkirk when I ran into the old duck of a mother waiting outside the big grey church, towards dusk.

But now she is sorrowful, poor dear, a cloud has come over her bright, generous face, with its affectionate black eyes, and tender lips.

"He has been ordered to the trenches near Ypres!" she whispers sadly.

"And your daughter," I gasp out.

"Hush! Here she comes. My angel, with the heart of a lion. She has been in the church to pray for him!   She would go alone."

Of our three faces it is still the girl wife's that is the brightest.

She has changed, of course.

She is no longer staring with dazzled eyes into her own bliss.

But the illumination of great love is there still, made doubly beautiful now by the knowledge that her beloved is out across those flat sand dunes, under shell-fire, and the time has come for her to be noble as a soldier's bride must be, for the sake of her husband's honour, and his little one unborn.

"Though he fall on the battle-field," she says to me softly, with that sweet, brave smile on her quivering lips, "he leaves me with a child to live after him, – his child!"

And of the three of us, it is she, the youngest and most sorely tried, who looks to have the greatest hold on life present and eternal.

CHAPTER LI

A LUCKY MEETING

To meet some one you know at the Front is an experiment in psychology, deeply interesting, amusing sometimes, and often strangely illuminative.

Indeed you never really know people till you meet them under the sound of guns.

It is at Furnes that I meet accidentally a very eminent journalist and a very well-known author.

Suddenly, up drives a funny old car with all its windows broken.

Clatter, clatter, over the age-old cobbled streets of Furnes, and the car comes to a stop before the ancient little Flemish Inn. Out jump four men. Hastening, like school-boys, up the steps, they come bursting breezily into the room where I have just finished luncheon.

Hook! They look!! We all look!!!

One of them with a bright smile comes forward.

"How do you do?" says he.

He is the chauffeur, if you please, the chauffeur in the big golden-brown overcoat, with a golden-brown hood over his head. He looks like a monk till you see his face. Then he is all brightness, and sharpness, and alertness. For in truth he is England's most famous War-Photographer, this young man in the cowl, with the hatchet profile and dancing green eyes, and we last saw each other in the agony of the Bombardment of Antwerp.

And then I look over his shoulder and see another face.

I can scarcely believe my eyes.

Here, at the world's end, as near the Front as anyone can get, driving about in that old car with the broken windows, is our eminent journalist, in baggy grey knee breeches and laced-up boots.

"Having a look round," says the journalist simply. "Seeing things for myself a bit!"

"How splendid!"

"Well, to tell you the truth, I can't keep away. I've been out before, but never so near as this. The sordidness and suffering of it all makes me feel I simply can't stay quietly over there in London. I want to see for myself how things are going."

Then, dropping the subject of himself swiftly, but easily, the journalist begins courteously to ask questions; what am I doing here? where have I come from? where am I going?

"Well, at the present moment," I answer, "I'm trying to get to La Panne. I want to see the Queen of the Belgians waiting for the King, and walking there on the yellow, dreamy sands by the North Sea. But the tram isn't running any longer, and the roads are bad to-day, very bad indeed!"

All in an instant, the journalistic instinct is alive in him, and crying. I watch, fascinated.

I can see him seeing that picture of pictures, the sweet Queen walking on the lonely winter sands, waiting for her hero to come back from the battlefields, just over there.

"Let us take you in our car! What are we doing? Where were we going ? Anyway, it doesn't matter. We'll take the car to La Panne! "

And after luncheon off we go.

Every now and then I turn the corner of my eye on the man beside me as he sits there, hunched up in a heavy coat with a big cigar between his babyish lips, talking, talking; and what is so glorious about it all is that this isn't the journalist talking, it is the idealist, the practical dreamer, who, by sheer belief in his ideals has won his way to the top of his profession.

I see a face that is one of the most curiously fascinating in Europe. A veiled face, but with its veil for ever shifting, for ever lifting, for ever letting you get a glimpse of the man behind. Power and will are sunk deep within the outer veil, and when you look at him at first you say to yourself, "What a nice big boy of a man!" For those lips are almost babyish in their curves, the lips of a man who would drink the cold pure water of life in preference to its coloured vintages, the lips of an idealist. Who but an idealist could keep a childish mouth through the intense worldliness of the battle for life as this man has fought it, right from the very beginning?

Over the broad, thoughtful brow flops a lock of brown hair every now and then. His eyes are grey with blue in them. When you look at them they look straight at you, but it is not a piercing glance. It seems like a glance from far away. All kinds of swift flashing thoughts and impulses go sweeping over those eyes, and what they don't see is really not worth seeing, though, when I come to think of it, I cannot recall catching them looking at anything. As far as faces go this is a fine face. Decidedly, a fine arresting face. Sympathetic, likeable. And the strong, well-made physique of a frame looks as if it could carry great physical burdens, though more exercise would probably do it good.

Above and beyond everything he looks young, this man; young with a youth that will never desert him, as though he holds within himself "the secrets of ever-recurring spring."

On we fly.

We are right inside the Belgian lines now; the Belgian soldiers are all around us, brave, wonderful *"Petits Beiges!"*

They always speak of themselves like that, the Belgian Army: "Les Petits Belges!"

Perhaps the fact that they have proved themselves heroes of an immortality that every race will love and bow down to in ages to come, makes these blue-coated men thus lightly refer to themselves, with that inimitable flash of the Belgian smile, as "little Belgians."

For never before was the Belgian Army greater than it is to-day, with its numbers depleted, its territory wrested from it, its homes ruined, its loved ones scattered far and wide in strange lands.

Like John Brown's Army it "still goes fighting on," though many of its uniforms, battered and stained with the blood and mud and powder of one campaign after another, are so ragged as to be almost in pieces.

"We are no longer chic!"

A Belgian Captain says it with a grin, as he chats to us at a halt where we shew our passes.

He flaps his hands in his pockets of his ragged overcoat and smiles.

In a way, it is true ! Their uniforms are ragged, stained, burnt, torn, too big, too little, full of a hundred pitiful little discrepancies that peep out under those brand new overcoats that some of them are lucky enough to have obtained. They have been fighting since the beginning of the War. They have left bits of their purple-blue tunics at Liege, Namur, Charleroi, Aerschot, Termonde, Antwerp. They have lost home, territory, family, friends. But they are fighting harder than ever. And so gloriously uplifted are they by the immortal honour they have wrested from destiny, that they can look at their ragged trousers with a grin, and love them, and their torn, burnt, blackened tunics, even as a cpnqueror loves the emblems of his glory that will never pale upon the pages of history.

A soldier loosens a bandage with his teeth, and breaks into a song.

It is so gay, so naive, so insouciant, so truly and deliciously Beige, that I catch it ere it fades, – that mocking song addressed to the Kaiser, asking, in horror, who are these ragged beings:

THE BELGIAN TO THE GERMAN

Ils n'ont pas votre bel tunique,
Et ils n'ont pas votre bel air
Mais leur courage est magnifique.
Si ils n'ont pas votre bel tunique!
A votre morgue ils donnent la nicque.
Au milieu de leur plus gros revers,

Si ils n'ont pas votre bel tunique,
Et ils n'ont pas votre bel air!

"What those poor fellows want most," says the journalist as we flash onwards, "is boots! They want one hundred thousand boots, the Belgian Army. You can give a friend all sorts of things. But he hardly likes it if you venture to give him boots. And yet they want them, these poor, splendid Belgians. They want them, and they must have them. We must give them to them somehow. Lots of them have no boots at all!"

"I heard that the Belgians were getting boots from America," the author puts in suddenly.

The journalist turns his head with a jerk.

"What do you mean," he asks sharply. "Do you mean that they have *ordered* them from America, or that America's *giving* them?"

"I believe what my informant, a sick officer in the Belgian Army, whom I visited this morning, told me was that the Americans were *giving* the boots."

"Are you sure it's *giving?*" the journalist persists. "We English ought to see to that. Last night I had an interview with the Belgian Minister of War and I tried to get on this subject of boots. But somehow I felt it was intrusive of me. I don't know. It's a delicate thing. It wants handling. Yet *they must have the boots."*

And I fancy they will get them, the heroes of Belgium. I think they will get their hundred thousand boots.

Then a whiff of the sea reaches us and the grey waves of the North Sea stretch out before us over the edge of the endless yellow sands, where bronze-faced Turcos are galloping their beautiful horses up and down.

We are in La Panne.

The journalist sits still in his corner of the car, not fussing, not questioning, leaving it all to me. This is my show. It is I who have come here to see the gracious Queen on the sands. All the part he plays in it is to bring me.

So the journalist, and the author and the others remain in the car. That is infinitely considerate, exquisitely so, indeed.

For no writer on earth would care to go looking around with the Jupiter of Journalists at her elbow!

* * * *

Rush, rush, we are on our way back now. The cold wind of wet, flat Flanders strikes at us as we fly along. It hits us in the face and on the back. It flicks us by the ear and by the throat. The window behind us is open. The window to right and the window to left are open too. All the windows are open because, as I said before, they are all broken!

In fact, there are no windows! They've all been smashed out of existence. There are only holes.

"We were under shell-fire this morning," observes the journalist contentedly. Then truthfully he adds, "I don't like shrapnel!"

Any woman who reads this will know how I felt in my pride when a malicious wind whisked my fur right off my shoulders, and flung it through the back window, far on the road behind.

If it hadn't been sable I would have let it go out of sheer humiliation.

But instead, after a moment's fierce struggle, remembering all the wardrobe I had already lost in Antwerp, I whispered gustily, "My stole! It's blown right out of the window."

How did I hope the journalist would not be cross, for we were racing back then against time, *without lights*, and it was highly important to get off these crowded roads with the soldiers coming and going, coming and going, before night fell.

Cross indeed!

I needn't have worried.

Absence of fuss, was, as I decided later, the most salient point about this man. In fact, his whole desire seemed to make himself into an entire nonentity. He never asserted himself. He never interfered. He never made any suggestions. He just sat quiet and calm in his corner of the car, puffing away at his big cigar.

Another curious thing about him was the way in which this man, used to bossing, organizing, suggesting, commanding, fell into his part, which was by force of circumstances a very minor one.

He was incognito. He was not the eminent journalist at all. He was just an eager man, out looking at a War. He was there, – in a manner of speaking, on suffrance. For in War time, civilians are *not* wanted at the Front! And nobody recognized this more acutely than the man with the cigar between his lips, and the short grey knee breeches showing sturdy legs in their dark grey stockings and thick laced-up boots.

The impression he gave me was of understanding absolutely the whole situation, and of a curiously technical comprehension of the wee little tiny part that he could be allowed to play.

"Where are you staying in Dunkirk ?"he asked."

"In a room over a milliner's shop. The town's full. I couldn't get in anywhere else."

"Then will you dine with us to-night at half-past seven, at the Hotel des Arcades ?"

"I should love to."

And we ran into Dunkirk.

And the lights flashed around me, and that extraordinary whirl of officers and men, moving up and down the cobbled streets, struck at us afresh, and we saw the sombre khaki of Englishmen, and the blue and red of the Belgian, and the varied uniforms and scarlet trousers of the Piou-Piou,[11] and the absolutely indescribable life and thrill and crowding of Dunkirk in these days, when the armies of three nations moved surging up and down the narrow streets.

---

[11] "Piou-piou" was the way French soldiers were called at the time of WW1. Some say it is derived from French "pion" ("pawn"), other say it's from chick's call, since French soldiers – as people said – were used to stole chicken from farms.

At seven-thirty I went up the wide staircase of the Hotel des Arcades in the Grand Place of Dunkirk. Quite a beautiful and splendid hotel though innumerable Taubes had sailed over it threatening to deface it with their ugly little bombs, but luckily without success so far, – very luckily indeed considering that every day at lunch or dinner some poor worn-out Belgian Officer came in there to get a meal.

Precisely half-past seven, and there hastening towards me was our host.

He had not "dressed," as we say in England. He had merely exchanged the short grey Norfolk knickerbockers for long trousers, and the morning coat for a short dark blue serge.

His eyes were sparkling.

"There's a Belgian here whom I want you to meet," he said in his boyish manner, that admirably concealed the power of this man that one was for ever forgetting in his presence, only to remember it all the more acutely when one thought of him afterwards. "It's the chief of the Belgian Medical Department. He's quite a wonderful man."

And we went in to dinner.

The journalist arranged the table.

It was rather an awkward one, numerically, and I was interested to see how he would come out of the problematic affair of four men and one woman.

But with one swift wave of his hand he assigned us to our places.

He sat on one side of the table with the Head of the Belgian Medical Corps at his right.

I sat opposite to him, and the author sat on my left, and the other man who had something to do with Boy Scouts on his left, and there we all were, and a more delightful dinner could not be imagined, for in a way it was exciting through the very fact of being eaten in a city that the Germans only the day before had pelted with twenty bombs.

Personalities come more clearly into evidence at dinner than at any other time, and so I was interested to see how the journalist played his part of host.

What would he be like?

There are so many different kinds of hosts. Would he be the all-see-
ing, all-reaching, all-divining kind, the kind that knows all you want,
and ought to want, and sees that you get it, the kind that says always
the right thing at the right moment, and keeps his party alive with his
sally of wit and gaiety, and bonhomie, and makes everyone feel that
they are having the time of their lives ?

No!

One quickly discovered that the journalist was not at all that kind
of host.

At dinner, where some men become bright and gay and inconse-
quential, this man became serious.

The food part of the affair bored him.

Watching him and studying him with that inner eye that makes the
bliss of solitude,[12] one saw he didn't care a bit about food, and still
less about wine. It wouldn't have mattered to him how bad the dinner was. He wouldn't know. He couldn't think about it. For he was
something more than your bon viveur and your social animal, this
man with his wide grey eyes and the flopping lock on his broad forehead. He was the dreamer of dreams as well as the journalist. And at
dinner he dreamed. Oh, yes, indeed, he dreamed tremendously. It
was all the same to him whether or not he ate paté de fois gras, or
fowl bouillé, or sausage. He was rapt in his discussion with the
Belgian Doctor on his right.

Anaesthetics and antiseptics, – that's what they are talking about so
hard.

And suddenly out comes a piece of paper.

The journalist wants to send a telegram to England.

"I'm going to try and get Doctor X. to come out here. He's a very
clever chap. He can go into the thing thoroughly. It's important. It
must be gone into."

---

[12] "They flash upon that inward eye / Which is the bliss of solitude", verses 21-22 from *I wandered lonely as a cloud* by William Wordsworth.

And there, on the white cloth, scribbled on the back of a menu, he writes out his telegram.

"But then," says the journalist, reflectively, "if I sign that the censor will hold it up for three days!"

The Head of the Belgian Medical Department smiles.

He knows what that telegram would mean to the Belgian Army.

"Let *me* sign it," he says in a gentle voice, "let me sign it and send it. My telegrams are not censored, and your English Doctor will meet us at Calais to-morrow, and all will be well with your magnificent idea !"

Just then the author on the left appears a trifle uneasy.

He holds up an empty Burgundy bottle towards the light.

"A dead 'un !" he announces, distinctly.

But our host, in his abstraction, does not hear.

The author picks up the other bottle, holds it to the light, screws up one eye at it, and places it lengthwise on the table.

"That's a dead 'un too," he says.

Just then, with great good luck, he manages to catch the journalist's grey eye.

"That's a dead 'un too,"he repeats loudly.

How exciting to see whether the author, in his quite natural desire to have a little more wine, will succeed in penetrating his host's dreaminess and absorption in the anæsthetics of the Belgian Army.

And then all of a sudden the journalist wakes up.

"Would you like some more wine?" he inquires.

"These are both dead 'uns," asserts the author courageously.

"We'll have some more !" says the journalist.

And more Burgundy comes ! But to the eminent journalist it is non-existent. For his mind is still filled with a hundred thousand things the Belgian Army want, – the iodine they need, and the anaesthetics. And nothing else exists for him at that moment but to do what he can for the nation that has laid down its life for England.

Burgundy, indeed!

And yet one feels glad that the author eventually gets his extra bottle. He has done something for England too. He has given us laughter when our days were very black.

And our soldiers love his yarns!

CHAPTER LII

THE RAVENING WOLF

How hard it must be for the soldiers to remember that there ever was Summer! How far off, how unreal are those burning, breathless days that saw the fighting round Namur, Termonde, Antwerp. Here in Flanders, in December, August and September seem to belong to centuries gone by.

Ugh! How cold it is!

The wind howls up and down this long, white, snow-covered road, and away on either side, as far as the eyes can see, stretches wide flat Flanders country, white and glistening, with the red sun sinking westward, and the pale little silvery moon smiling her pale little smile through the black bare woods.

In this little old Flemish village from somewhere across the snow the thunder and fury of terrific fighting makes sleep impossible for more than five minutes at a time.

Then suddenly something wakes me, and I know at once, even before I am quite awake, that it is not shell-fire this time.

What is it?

I sit up in bed, and feel for the matches.

But before I can strike one I hear again that extraordinary and very horrible sound.

I lie quite still.

And now a strange thing has happened.

In a flash my thoughts have gone back over years and years and years, and it is twenty-eight years ago and I have crossed thousands and thousands of "loping leagues of sea," [13] and am in Australia, in the burning heat of mid-summer. I am a schoolgirl spending my Christmas holidays in the Australian bush. It is night. I am a nervous little highly-strung creature. A noise wakes me. I shriek and wake the household. When they come dashing in I sob out pitifully.

"There's a wolf outside the window, I heard it howling!"

"It's only a dingo, darling !" says a woman's tender voice, consolingly. "It's only a native dog trying to find water! It can't get in here anyway."

I remember too, that I was on the ground floor then, and I am on the ground floor now, and I find myself wishing I could hear that comforting voice again, telling me this is only a dingo, this horrible howling thing outside there in the night.

I creep out of bed, and tiptoe to the window.

Quite plainly in the silvery moonlight I see, standing in the wide open space in front of this little Flemish Inn, a thin gaunt animal with its tongue lolling out. I see the froth on the tongue, and the yellow-white of its fangs glistening in the winter moonlight. I ask myself what is it? And I ask too why should I feel so frightened ? For I *am* frightened. From behind the white muslin curtains I gaze at that apparition, absolutely petrified.

It seems to me that I shall never, never, never be able to move again when I find myself knocking at the Caspiar's door, and next minute the old proprietor of the Inn and his wife are peeping through my window.

"Mon Dieu ! It is a wolf!"

Old Caspiar frames the word with his lips rather than utter them.

"You must shoot it," frames his wife.

Old Caspiar gets down his gun.

But it falls from his hands.

"I can't shoot any more,"he groans. "I've lost my nerve."

He begins to cry.

[13] Verse from *Written in Australia* by Australian poet Arthur H. Adams.

Poor old man!

He has lost a son, eleven nephews, and four grandsons in this War, as well as his nerve. Poor old chap. And he remembers the siege of Paris, he remembers only too well that terrible, far-off, unreal, dreamlike time that has suddenly leapt up out of the dim, far past into the present, shedding its airs of unreality, and clothing itself in all the glaring horrors of to-day, until again the Past is the Present, and the Present is the Past, and both are inextricably and cruelly mixed for Frenchmen of Caspiar's age and memories.

A touch on my arm and I start violently.

"Madame!"

It is poor old Madame Caspiar whispering to *me*.

"You are English. You are brave n'est-ce-pas ? Can *you* shoot the wolf."

I am staggered at the idea.

"Shoot! Oh ! I'd miss it! I daren't try it. I've never even handled a gun!" I stammer out.

I see myself revealed now as the coward that I am.

"Then *I* shall shoot it!" says old Madame Caspiar in a trembling voice.

She picks up the gun.

"When I was a girl I was a very good shot!"

She speaks loudly, as if to reassure herself.

Old Caspiar suddenly jumps up.

"You're mad, Terese. Vous êtes folle ! You can't even see to read the newspapers, *You!*"

He takes the gun from her!

She begins to cry now.

"I shall go and call the others," she says, weeping.

"Be quiet," he says crossly. "You'll frighten the beast away if you make a noise like that!"

He crosses the room and peers out again!

"It's eating something!" he says. "Mon Dieu ! *It's got* Chou-chou."

Chou-chou is – *was* rather, the Caspiar's pet rabbit.

"You shall pay for that!" mutters old Caspiar.

Gently opening the window, he fires.

* * * *

"Not since 1860 have I seen a wolf," says Caspiar, looking down at the dead beast. "Then they used to run in out of the forest when I was an apprentice in my uncle's Inn. We were always frightened of them. And now, even after the Germans, we are frightened of them still."

"I am more frightened of wolves than I am of Germans," confesses Madame Caspiar in a whisper.

We stand there in the breaking dawn, looking at the dead wolf, and wondering fearfully if there are not more of its kind, creeping in from the snow-filled plains beyond.

Other figures join us.

Two Red-Cross French doctors, a wounded English Colonel, la grandmère, Mme. Caspiar's mother, and a Belgian priest, all come issuing gradually from the low portals of the Inn into the yard.

Then in the chill dawn, with the glare of the snow-fields in our eyes, we discuss the matter in low voices.

It is touching to find that each one is thinking of his own country's soldiers, and the menace that packs of hungry wolves may mean to them, English, Belgian, French; especially to wounded men.

"It's the sound of the guns that brings them out," says a Krench doctor learnedly. "This wolf has probably travelled hundreds of miles. And of course there are more. Oui, oui! C'est ca! Certainly there will be more."

"C'est ca, c'est ca!" agrees the priest.

"Such a huge beast too!" says the Colonel.

He is probably comparing it with a fox.

I find myself mentally agreeing with Madame Caspiar that Germans are really preferable to wolves.

The long, white, snow-covered road that leads back to the world seems endlessly long as I stare out of the Inn windows realizing that sooner or later I must traverse that long white lonely road across the plains before I can get to safety, and the nearest town. Are there more wolves in there, slinking ever nearer to the cities ? That is what everyone seems to believe now. We see them in scores, in hundreds, prowling with hot breath in search of wounded soldiers, or anyone they can get.

We are all undoubtedly depressed.

Then a Provision "Motor" comes down that road, and out of it jumps a little, old, white-mous-tached man in a heavy sheepskin overcoat and red woollen gloves, carrying something wrapped in a shawl.

He comes clattering into the Inn.

His small black eyes are swimming with tears.

"Mon Dieu!" he says, gulping some coffee and rum. "Give me a little hot milk, Madame ! My poor monkey is near dying."

A tiny, black, piteous face looks out of the shawl, and huskily the man with the red gloves explains that he has been for weeks trying to get his travelling circus out of the danger-zone.

"The Army commandeered my horses. We had great difficulty in moving about. We wanted to get to Paris. All my poor animals have been terrified by the noises of the big guns. Especially the monkeys. They've all died except this one."

"You poor little beast!"says the Colonel, bending down.

He has seen men die in thousands, this gaunt Englishman with his eye in a sling.

But his voice is infinitely compassionate as he looks with one eye at the little shivering creature, and murmurs again, "You *poor* little brute!"

"Yesterday," adds the man with the red gloves, "my trick wolf escaped. She was a beauty, and so clever. When the War began I used to dress her up as a French solider, – red trousers, red cap and all! *I s'pose you haven't seen a wolf, M'sieur, running about these parts?"*

Nobody answers for a bit.

We are all stunned.

* * * *

But the old fellow brightens up when he hears that his wolf ate the rabbit.

"Ah, but she was a clever wolf!" he cries excitedly. "Very likely the reason why she ate your Chou-chou was because she has played the part of a French soldier. *French soldiers always steal the rabbits!*"

CHAPTER LIII

BACK TO LONDON

I am on my way back to London, grateful and glad to be once more on our side of the Channel.

"Five days!" exclaims a young soldier in the train.

He flings back his head, draws a deep breath, and remains staring like an imbecile at the roof of the railway carriage for quite two minutes.

Then he shakes himself, draws another deep breath, and says again, still staring at the roof:

"Five days!"

The train has started now out into the night. We have left Folkestone well behind. We have pulled down all the blinds because a proclamation commands us to do so, and we are softly, yet swiftly rushing through the cool, sweet-smelling English country back towards good old Victoria Station, where all continental trains must now make their arrivals and departures.

"Have you been wounded, Sir?" asks an old lady in a queer black astrakhan cap, and with a big nose.

"Wounded? Rather! Right on top of the head." He ducks his fair head to shew us. "I didn't know it when it happened. I didn't feel anything at all. I only knew there was something wet. Blood, I suppose. Then they sent me to the Hospital at S. Lazaire, and I had a ripping Cornish nurse. But lor, what a fool I was! I actually signed on that I wanted to go back. Why did I do that? I don't know. I didn't want to go back. *Want to go back?* Good lor! Think of it! But I went back! and the next thing was Mons! [14] Even now I can't believe it, that march.

The Germans were at us all the time. It didn't seem possible we could do it. ' Buck up, men! only another six kilometres!' an officer would say. Then it would be: 'Only another seven kilometres! keep going, men!' Sometimes we went to sleep marching and woke up and found ourselves still marching. Always we were shifting and relieving. It was a wonderful business. It seemed as if we were done for. It seemed as if we couldn't go on. But we did. Good lor! *We did it!* Somehow the English generally seem to do it. Some of us had no boots left. Some of us had no feet. *But WE DID IT!*"

The old lady with the black astrakhan cap nods vigorously.

"And the Germans wouldn't acknowledge that victory of ours," she says ! "I didn't see it in any of their papers."

It is rather lovely to hear the dear creature alluding to Mons as "our victory!"

But indeed she is right. Mons is, in truth, our glory and our pride!

But it is still more startling to find she knows secret things about the German newspapers, and we all look at her sharply.

"I've just come from Germany!" the old lady explains. "Just come from Dresden, where I've been living for fifteen years. Oh dear ! I did have a time getting away. But I had to leave ! They made me. *Dresden is being turned into a fortified town and a basis for operations!*"

We all now listen to *her*, the soldiers three as well.

"Whenever we heard a noise in Dresden, everyone said, 'It's the Russians coming!' So you see how frightened they are of the Russians. They are scared to death. They've almost forgotten their hatred for England. They talk of nothing now but the Russians. Their terror is really pathetic, considering all the boasting they've been doing up to now. They made a law that no one was to put his head out of the window under *pain of death!*"

"Beasts!" says the wounded one.

"There's only military music in Dresden now. All the theatres and concert rooms are shut. And of course from now there will be nothing

14 The Battle of Mons (23 August 1914).

but military doings in Dresden ! Yes, I lived there for fifteen years. I tried to stay on. I had many English friends as well as Germans, and the English all agreed to taboo all English people who adopted a pro-German tone. Some did, but not many. My greatest friends, my dearest friends were Germans. But the situation grew impossible for us all. We were not alienated personally, but we all knew that there would come between us something too deep and strong to be defied or denied, even for great affection's sake. So I cut the cables and left when the order was given that Dresden was henceforth to be a fortified town. Besides, it was dangerous for me to remain. I was English, and they hissed at me sometimes when I went out. It was through the American Consul's assistance that I was enabled to get away. I saw such horrid pictures of the English in all the shops. It made my blood boil. I saw one picture of the Englishmen with *three legs to run away with!*"

"Beasts!" says the wounded one. "Wait till I travel in Germany!"

"And, oh dear!" goes on the old lady, "I was so frightened that I should forget and put my head out without thinking ! As I sat in the train coming away from Dresden, I said to myself all the time, ' You must not look out of the window, or you'll have your head shot off ! ' That was because they feared the Russian spies might try to drop explosives out of the trains on to their bridges!"

"Beasts!" says the wounded one again.

It is really remarkable what a variety of expressions this fair-haired young English gentleman manages to put in a word.

He belongs to a good family and at the beginning of the War he cleared out without a word to anyone and enlisted in the ranks. Now he is coming home on five days' leave, covered with glory and a big scar, to get his commission. He is a splendid type. All he thinks about is his Country, and killing Germans. He is a gorgeous and magnificent type, for here he is in perfect comradeship with his pal Tommy[15] in the corner, and the Irishman next to him. Evidently to him they

---

[15] "Tommy Atkins" (often just "Tommy") is slang for a common soldier in the British Army, very popular during WW1.

are more than gentlemen. They are men who've been with him through Mons, and the Battle of the Aisne, and the Battle of Ypres, and he loves them-for what they are! And they love him for what he is, and they're a splendid trio, the soldiers three.

"When I git into Germany," says Tommy, "I mean to lay hands on all I can git! I'm goin' to loot off them Germans, like they looted off them pore Beljins!"

"Surely you wouldn't be like the Crown Prince," says the old lady, and we all wake up to the fact then that she's really a delightful old lady, for only a delightful old lady could put the case as neatly as that.

"Shure, all I care about," says the big, quiet Irishman in the corner, "is to sleep and sleep and sleep!"

"On a bed," says the wounded one. "Good lor! Think of it! To-night I'll sleep in a bed. I'll roll over and over to make sure I'm there. Think of it, sheets, blankets. We don't even get a blanket in the trenches. We might get too comfortable and go to sleep."

"What about the little oil stoves the newspapers say you're having?" asks the old lady.

"We've seen none of them!" assert the soldiers three.

"Divil a one of them," adds the Irishman.

"I've eat things I never eat before," says Tommy suddenly, in his simple way that is so curiously telling. "I've eat raw turnips out of the fields. They're all eatin' raw turnips over there. And I've eat sweets. I've eat pounds of chocolates if I could get them and I've never eat them before in my life sinst I was a kid."

"Oh, chocolates!" says the wounded one, ecstatically. "But chocolate in the sheet – thick, wide, heavy chocolate – there's nothing on earth like it! I wrote home, and put all over my letters, Chocolate, *chocolate*, CHOCOLATE. They sent me out tons of it. But I never got it. It went astray, somewhere or other."

"But they're very good to us," says Tommy earnestly. "We don't want for no thin'. You couldn't be better treated than what we are!"

"What do you like most to receive?" asks the old lady.

"Chocolate," they all answer simultaneously.

"The other night at Ypres," says Tommy with his usual unexpect-
edness, "a German came out of his trenches. He shouted: 'German
waiter! want to come back to the English. Please take me prisoner.'
We didn't want no German waiters. We can't be bothered takin' the
beggars prisoners. We let go at him instead!"

"They eat like savages!" puts in the Irishman. "I've see them shov-
elling their food in with one hand and pushing it down with the
other. 'Tis my opinion the Germans have got no throats!"

"The Germans have lots to eat," asserts Tommy. "Whenever we
capture them we always find them well stocked. Brown bread. They
always have brown bread, and bully beef, and raisins."

"Beasts!" says the wounded one again. "But good lor, their Jack
Johnsons! [16] When I think of them now I can't believe it at all.
They're like fifty shells a minute sometimes. Sometimes in the middle of all the inferno I'd think I was dead? or in hell. I often thought
that."

"Them guns cawst them a lot," says Tommy. "It cawst £250 each
loading. We used to be laying there in the trenches and to pass the
time while they was firing at us we'd count up how much it was caw-
sting them. That's 17s. 6d., that bit of shrapnel! we'd say. And there
goes another £5! They waste their shells something terrible too.
There's thirty five-pound notes gone for nothing we'd reckon up
sometimes when thirty shells had exploded in nothin' but mud!"

Then the wounded one tells us a funny story.

"I was getting messages in one day when this came through: '*The
Turks are wearing fez and neutral trousers!*' We couldn't make head or
tail of the neutral trousers ! So we pressed for an explanation. It came.
'*The Turks are wearing fez, breaches of neutrality!*'"

---

[16] "Jack Johnson" (1878 – 1946) was the first Afro-American world heavyweight boxing
champion. During WW1, it was also a British nickname for a German 15-cm artillery shell.

* * * *

And while we are laughing the train runs into Victoria Station and the soldiers three leap joyously out into the rain-wet London night.

Then dear familiar words break on our ears, in a woman's voice.

"Any luggage, Mum!" says a woman porter.

And we know that old England is carrying on as usual!

THE END

CONTENTS

13   I – Crossing the Channel

17   II – On the way to Antwerp

23   III – Germans on the line

29   IV – In the tracks of the Huns

35   V – Aerschot

40   VI – The swift retribution

41   VII – They would not kill the cook

42   VIII – "You'll never get there"

47   IX – Setting out on the great adventure

50   X – From Ghent to Grammont

58   XI – Brabant

60   XII – Driving extraordinary

66   XIII – The lunch at Enghien

69   XIV – We meet the grey-coats

71   XV – Face to face with the Huns

75   XVI – A prayer for his soul

77   XVII – Brussels

80   XVIII – Burgomaster Max

87   XIX – His arrest

89   XX – General Thys

92   XXI – How Max has influenced Brussels

95   XXII – Under German occupation

100   XXIII – Chanson triste

101   XXIV – The cult of the Brute

104   XXV – Death in life

109   XXVI – The return from Brussels

114   XXVII – "The English are coming"

117   XXVIII – Monday

120   XXIX – Tuesday

123   XXX – Wednesday

127   XXXI – The city is shelled

133   XXXII – Thursday

136   XXXIII – The endless day

138   XXXIV – I decide to stay

140   XXXV – The city surrenders

147   XXXVI – A solitary walk

152   XXXVII – Enter les Allemands

154   XXXVIII – "My son!"

155   XXXIX – The reception

156   XL – The laughter of brutes

158   XLI – Traitors

161   XLII – What the waiting maid saw

166   XLIII – Saturday

176   XLIV – Can I trust them?

183   XLV – A safe shelter

188   XLVI – The flight into Holland

191   XLVII – Friendly Holland

197   XLVIII – French cooking in war time

202   XLIX – The fight in the air

206   L – The war bride

211   LI – A lucky meeting

222   LII – The ravening wolf

228   LIII – Back to London

Printed by
On-Demand Publishing, LLC
Scotts Valley, CA 95066 United States

34032019R00139

Printed in Great Britain
by Amazon